WRESTLING
MANIAC'S
SUPER TRIVIA

Brendan O'Neill

With special thanks to Steve Anderson

WINDING
STAIR
PRESS

National Library of Canada Cataloguing in Publication Data

O'Neill, Brendan
        Wrestling maniac's super trivia

ISBN 1-55366-253-9

        I. Wrestling – Miscellanea. II. Title.
GV1195.054 2002   796.812   C2002-900261-3

Winding Stair Press
An imprint of Stewart House Publishing Inc.
Etobicoke, Ontario
www.stewarthousepub.com
Executive Vice President and Publisher: Ken Proctor
Director of Publishing and Product Acquisition: Joe March
Production Manager: Ruth Bradley-St-Cyr
Cover design: Darrin Laframboise
Book design: Susan Paterson

Printed and bound in Canada

Photo credits in page order:
Cover: Dr. Michael Lano. viii: George Napolitano. 4: Bill Janosik. 20:
George Napolitano. 26: Dr. Michael Lano. 32: Bob Leonard. 54: Bob
Leonard. 72: Dr. Michael Lano. 102: Dr. Michael Lano.

CONTENTS

INTRODUCTION

Professional wrestling has been around in one form or another for more than 100 years, since the mid- to late 1800s. Although its beginnings are unclear and its actual origin a bit muddied, many believe that the type of wrestling which evolved into today's pro wrestling started in carnivals. The resident "carnie" toughman challenged all comers to wrestle him, with the purpose either to beat the carnie or even last 10 minutes.

From then on, wrestling became more and more common, growing in popularity to the point that "regular" folk engaged in competitions, and even some of the most influential people of the time dabbled in wrestling. A number of U.S. presidents have a wrestling background; can you name them?

With that simple question, the idea for this book was born. Professional wrestling has such a storied, fascinating past and present – one that compares favorably to all of the four "major" sports (football, basketball, baseball and hockey). When the subject of pro wrestling comes up in discussions at the local tavern or around the office water cooler, inevitably interesting questions are thrown about with some surprising, unusual answers.

Our goal was to compile the most comprehensive book of wrestling trivia questions, and after reading *Wrestling Maniac's Trivia Book*, we hope you agree that we succeeded. But once we collected and created hundreds and hundreds of great wrestling trivia questions, we didn't know just how to put them together. So, we broke up the mass of questions into six basic sections: Old School, International, The Name Game, WWF, WCW and Miscellaneous. These categories encompass every type of question we could think of, from the most ridiculous gimmicks of wrestlers in the 1940s to the winningest wrestlers in the international circuits, to the heights and weights of today's stars in the powerhouse federations.

Pro wrestling's history has such a long, winding path, we didn't know where to start, so we started at the beginning. We compiled a wide variety of compelling trivia questions about the biggest and best wrestlers of the early days of pro wrestling, all the way back to 1871, through to the 1980s classics.

In this book you'll read about legendary champions of yesteryear like

1

"Peerless" Frank Gotch and the menacing Killer Kowalski, who once tore off Yukon Eric's ear. How about some fascinating facts about legends like Lou Thesz, who once held the heavyweight championship for 18 years? And of course, how can anyone talk about the best of old school wrestling without mentioning "The Human Orchid," Gorgeous George, who revolutionized the showmanship aspect of professional wrestling and was the predecessor to flamboyant stars like Ravishing Rick Rude and Goldust.

The history of pro wrestling also owes a great debt to wrestlers outside of North America. Knowing this, we chronicle the feats of the international scene from Japan's Antonio Inoki to Mexico's Tito Santana and Rey Misterio Jr. and New Zealand's Bushwhackers. We've even included the foreign wrestler for whom Madison Square Garden lifted its ban on masked wrestlers in 1972. Need a hint? Don't know who it was? Check out the International section for the answer.

In our research, we came across a grouping of questions that yield some of the funniest, most interesting answers. We call that section The Name Game. Basically, we tell you which wrestlers wrestled under names other than the moniker by which most of the world knows them. Did you know that Brutus Beefcake also went by the name Zodiac? Did you know that Randy "Macho Man" Savage was once known as The Spider? Also, we tell you the real names of your favorite wrestling stars. Sure, everyone knows Mankind is Mick Foley, but do you know the real name of Sid Vicious? We do, and if you want to know the answer, check out our Name Game section on page 25.

All this leads to the two big players in pro wrestling today and over the past 15 years – the WWF and WCW. In talking about these monsters of pro wrestling promotion, we discussed the greatest wrestlers and matches in the illustrious history of wrestling's largest federations. To start, we've compiled all sorts of questions and tidbits about the WWF. Here's just a taste: Who defeated Hulk Hogan in 1990 at WrestleMania 6 to win the WWF title? Answer: The Ultimate Warrior. Where is the WWF headquarters? Answer: Stamford, Connecticut. Who won the ladder match in 1994 at WrestleMania X between Razor Ramon and Shawn Michaels for the Intercontinental title? Answer: Razor Ramon.

But we don't discriminate against the WCW. Here are just a few of our WCW questions: How many times has Rey Misterio, Jr. won the WCW cruiserweight title? Answer: Five times. Who was WCW Rookie of the Year in 1997? Answer: Prince Iaukea. What is the name of Buff Bagwell's finishing move? Answer: The Buff Blockbuster.

And finally, when we came across questions that didn't easily fit into a category, we packed them all into one section and called it Miscellaneous. Here you'll find everything from lists of who's related to who in pro wrestling to questions about foreign objects and animals that were brought into the ring. Example: What type of bird did Koko B. Ware bring into the ring and dance with before each match? Answer: A cockatoo. What piece of dinnerware does Abdullah the Butcher most often use to scratch and cut his head? Answer: A fork. This section is filled with all sorts of trivia and facts about the more interesting aspects of wrestling as "sports entertainment."

Wrestling Maniac's Trivia Book exposes you to every aspect of pro wrestling, from its days as a brutal back-room sport to today's reign as the number one sports entertainment draw on the planet. Tens of millions of people attend pro wrestling events each year, watch it on television each week, and talk about it with their friends each day. Our hope is that this book will help enliven those discussions and arm our readers with the ammunition they need to stump their friends and baffle even the most knowledgeable wrestling fan.

OLD SCHOOL

Wrestling in one form or another is as old as civilization, dating back as far as the ancient Egyptians, according to some. But then wrestling came to America as immigrants came to the "New World" and a new type of sports entertainment was born.

Thanks to traveling carnivals and county fairs through the northeast, it is said that Vermont was the capital of the new wrestling "movement" in the 1700s.

While the sensational and sometimes barbaric sport of wrestling developed over the next 200 years, it became apparent that audiences all over the United States loved professional wrestling and fans flocked to see live events and watch matches on cable television.

The frenzy around wrestling reached its heyday in what people often call "The Golden Age of Wrestling," the 1940s-1980s. During this period wrestling grew in fits and starts, but developed a foothold in the American culture thanks to outlandish characters, amazing athleticism and shrewd marketing and promotion.

Today, in remembering the groundbreaking wrestlers and memorable matches of that day, we refer to it as "old school" wrestling. What this means is that it's all things that happened around 20 years ago...or more. But those "good ol' days" produced some of the best pro wrestling trivia questions we could think of.

Some great old school wrestlers include Gorgeous George, Killer Kawalski, The Crusher, The Bruiser, Andre the Giant, Big John Studd and Jimmy "Superfly" Snuka. These are the forefathers of today's young superstars, and fill our childhood memories with the sights and sounds of the first Battle Royal, WrestleMania 1, the time Andre slammed Big John Studd, or the time Jimmy "Superfly" Snuka jumped off the top of a cage, etc.

These old school wrestlers are the reason many of us got hooked on professional wrestling at an early age, and they laid the groundwork for the popularity of today's wrestlers. There would be no Mick Foley without Jimmy "Superfly" Snuka, no Paul Wight without Andre the Giant, and no Chyna without the Fabulous Moolah.

1. Which 1940s wrestler used a gimmick including being wheeled to the ring inside a cage and "released" by his handlers?
   A. The Tiger
   B. The Animal
   C. The Crazy Man
   D. The Gorilla

2. Which wrestler claimed he never lost a Battle Royal?
   A. Hulk Hogan
   B. King Kong Bundy
   C. Andre the Giant
   D. Jerry "The King" Lawler

3. Which 1950s wrestler appeared in a number of films directed by the infamous Ed Wood?
   A. Dick the Bruiser
   B. Tor Johnson
   C. Killer Kowalski
   D. Gorgeous George

4. How many world titles has Ric Flair won in the WWF and WCW since 1981?
   A. 17
   B. 20
   C. 18
   D. 14

5. Mildred Burke was the first great woman wrestler. In the 1930s she wrestled more than 200 men. How many of those matches did she lose?
   A. 3
   B. 10
   C. 1
   D. All of them
   E. None of them

6. What was the name of 1980s wrestler Lord Alfred Hayes' finishing move?
   A. The Lord's Leap
   B. London Bridge
   C. The Royal Kick
   D. The British Butt

7. How many times did Jerry Lawler win the United States Wrestling Association's heavyweight title?
   A. 40 times
   B. 19 times
   C. 34 times
   D. 26 times

8. What was the famous, nearly unstoppable signature move of Baron Von Raschke?
   A. The Kraut Klaw
   B. The Bratwurst Bump
   C. The German Claw
   D. The German Dropkick

9. With whom did Baron Von Raschke team to win the AWA World Tag Team Title in 1983?
   A. The Bruiser
   B. The Crusher
   C. Hans Schmidt
   D. Fritz Von Erich

10. True or False: Nikolai Volkoff once defeated legendary WWF title-holder Bruno Sammartino?

11. What was the finishing move of Chief Jay Strongbow in the 1970s and 80s?
    A. The Strongbow Backbreaker
    B. The Scalp
    C. The Peacepipe
    D. The Indian Sleeper

12. Lou Thesz is a wrestling legend with one of the longest careers ever. While he held titles in the 1960s, what year did he win his first world title?
    A. 1920
    B. 1959
    C. 1937
    D. 1946

13. Which 1950s wrestler competed well into his sixties and died from a fatal weightlifting injury?
    A. Dick the Bruiser
    B. Gorgeous George
    C. Hans Schmidt
    D. The Crusher

14. Which wrestler was the first Intercontinental Champion in 1979 and also won the WWF Hardcore title in 2000 at age 58?
    A. Jimmy "Superfly" Snuka
    B. Ric Flair
    C. Pat Patterson
    D. Jerry "The King" Lawler

15. Which wrestler was also known as "The Chest" because of his 63-inch chest (when expanded)?
    A. Barney Bernard
    B. The Wall
    C. Haystacks Callhoun
    D. The Giant Baba

16. In the "old days," what was the name for a wrestler who had great ability combined with some old wrestling tricks?
    A. A grappler
    B. A hooker
    C. A shooter
    D. A tricker

17. In the "old days," what was the name for a skilled, technically proficient wrestler, or scientific wrestler?
    A. A techie
    B. A tricker
    C. A shooter
    D. A grappler

18. Which of the following former U.S. presidents DID NOT wrestle prior to their political careers?
    A. George Washington
    B. Abraham Lincoln
    C. Teddy Roosevelt
    D. John F. Kennedy
    E. Zachary Taylor
    F. William Howard Taft
    G. Calvin Coolidge

19. In what year was the earliest recorded championship wrestling match in "The New World" held?
    A. 1871
    B. 1852
    C. 1874

D. 1902

20. What was that match called?
    A. The New World Championship for $1,000
    B. The Clash of the Colonies
    C. The Championship of the United States and Canada for $2,000
    D. The Championship of North America

21. Which old school wrestler had the nickname "Peerless" because he was thought to be unbeatable?
    A. Vern Gagne
    B. Frank Gotch
    C. Lou Thesz
    D. Bruno Sammartino

22. During the Depression, Jim Londos was one of wrestling's biggest draws. He pulled in a gate of $86,000 versus "Strangler" Lewis in 1934. Where was that match held?
    A. Madison Square Garden
    B. Boston Garden
    C. Fenway Park
    D. Wrigley Field

23. Which wrestler used to light cigars with $50 bills but then died broke at the age of 46?
    A. Gorgeous George
    B. Lou Thesz
    C. Verne Gagne
    D. Bruiser Brody

24. Which wrestler played the part of Tor Johnson in the 1994 film *Ed Wood*?
    A. George "The Animal" Steele
    B. King Kong Bundy
    C. "Superstar" Billy Graham
    D. Hillbilly Jim

25. What year did Captain Lou Albano join forces with Vince McMahon, Sr.?
    A. 1948
    B. 1963
    C. 1952
    D. 1971

26. What was the name of the wrestling organization founded by Vince McMahon, Sr. that eventually turned into the WWF?
    A. WOWF
    B. WWWF
    C. WOW
    D. WF

27. In what year did Vince McMahon, Sr. sell his interest in the WWF to his son?
    A. 1981
    B. 1983
    C. 1984
    D. 1987

28. Which wrestling organization, owned by Jim Crockett, became the NWA after the rest of the NWA promoters caved under the pressure of the WWF?
    A. Eastern Championship Wrestling
    B. American Wrestling Association
    C. Georgia Championship Wrestling
    D. American Wrestling Federation

29. Which wrestler tore off Yukon Eric's cauliflower ear?
    A. Gorgeous George
    B. The Cruiser
    C. Dick The Bruiser
    D. Killer Kowalski

30. What was the signature move of Robert Friedrich, a.k.a. "The Strangler"?
    A. Headlock
    B. Chokehold
    C. The Claw
    D. Full-nelson

31. Which 1930s wrestler is credited with executing the first "sleeper hold"?
    A. Antonio Rocca
    B. Bruno Sammartino
    C. Fritz Von Erich
    D. Jim Londos

32. Which 1950s-1970s wrestler held the heavyweight championship for 18 years?
    A. Verne Gagne

B. Lou Thesz
C. Frank Gotch
D. Jim Londos

33. Who was known as "The Human Orchid"?
    A. Verne Gagne
    B. Lou Thesz
    C. Gorgeous George
    D. Frank Gotch

34. Marvin Mercer's signature move was called an "Atomic Dropkick."
    What was special about this kick?
    A. He would dropkick his opponents and land back on his feet
    B. He dropkicked opponents from the top rope
    C. He used both feet
    D. He dropkicked them facing backwards

35. What was 1940s and 50s wrestler Antonio Rocca's signature move?
    A. The Italian Tank
    B. The Spanish Fly
    C. The Portuguese Punisher
    D. The Argentine Backbreaker

36. Andre the Giant was also called "The Eighth Wonder of the World."
    From where was this nickname taken?
    A. The comic book *Superman*
    B. The novel *Ulysses*
    C. The movie *King Kong*
    D. The book Dante's *Inferno*

37. Which wrestler held a world title every year from 1981 to 1996?
    A. Ric "Nature Boy" Flair
    B. Hulk Hogan
    C. Tito Santana
    D. Ricky "The Dragon" Steamboat

38. Which brothers are the only siblings to each be NWA world champions?
    A. Lanny Poffo and Randy Savage
    B. Bret Hart and Owen Hart
    C. Dory Funk, Jr. and Terry Funk
    D. Rick Steiner and Scott Steiner

39. What was the name of Fritz Von Erich's signature move?
    A. The German Potato Salad
    B. The Iron Claw
    C. The Steel Trap
    D. The Vise Grip

40. What was Dusty Rhodes' finishing move?
    A. The flying knee
    B. The leg drop
    C. The head butt
    D. The Bionic Elbow

41. On May 19, 1946, Andre the Giant was born in:
    A. Helsinki, Finland
    B. Oslo, Norway
    C. Munich, Germany
    D. Grenoble, France

42. What country did Maurice "Mad Dog" Vachon represent in the 1948 Olympic Games?
    A. Canada
    B. France
    C. USA
    D. Germany

43. Who did Verne Gagne defeat in his pro debut on April 18, 1949?
    A. Lou Thesz
    B. Abe Kashey
    C. Buddy Rogers
    D. Ray Steele

44. Which one of these men did not hold the AWA World tag team title with Verne Gagne?
    A. Crusher
    B. Moose Evans
    C. Bill Robinson
    D. Leo Nomellini

45. Following Boris Zukhov's jump to the WWF, who replaced him as Soldat Ustinov's partner and AWA tag team champion?
    A. Doug Somers
    B. Nikolai Volkoff
    C. Buddy Rose

D. Nick Kiniski

46. Who defeated Pat Patterson, the first WWF Intercontinental champion, for the title?
    A. Don Muraco
    B. Ken Patera
    C. Greg Valentine
    D. Pedro Morales

47. Who was crowned the first Universal Wrestling Federation (Bill Watts) champion?
    A. Steve Williams
    B. Terry Gordy
    C. One Man Gang
    D. Ted DiBiase

48. Who was the first "Triple Crown" champion (world, Intercontinental and tag team titles) in the WWF?
    A. Pedro Morales
    B. Bob Backlund
    C. Bruno Sammartino
    D. Buddy Rogers

49. What did Larry Zbyszko buy from Killer Brooks for $25,000 in 1983?
    A. Managerial Services
    B. Tournament Bye
    C. NWA National title
    D. A Tag Team

50. What was the name of the WWF's inaugural pay-per-view?
    A. Wrestlemania
    B. Royal Rumble
    C. War To Settle The Score
    D. The Wrestling Classic

51. Who did Adrian Adonis and Dick Murdoch defeat for the WWF World tag team title in 1984?
    A. The Wild Samoans
    B. Tony Atlas and Rocky Johnson
    C. The Moondogs
    D. Barry Windham and Mike Rotundo

52. Who replaced Barry Windham as Mike Rotundo's tag team partner in the WWF?

53. Who won the Wrestling Classic tournament in November of 1985?
A. Junkyard Dog
B. Randy Savage
C. Roddy Piper
D. Paul Orndorff

54. In response to the WWF's "invasion," the AWA and NWA teamed up to create what television program in the mid-eighties?
A. Pro Wrestling America
B. AWA/NWA Championship Wrestling
C. Ultimate Professional Wrestling
D. Pro Wrestling USA

55. What was the name of the MTV broadcast that launched "Rock-N-Wrestling"?
A. The War To Settle The Score
B. The Brawl For It All
C. The Rock and Wrestling Connection
D. Prelude To Wrestlemania

56. Which talk show host was injured by Hulk Hogan during a broadcast of his show?
A. Regis Philbin
B. Arsenio Hall
C. Richard Belzer
D. Rick Dees

57. Who was not an animated character on Hulk Hogan's *Rock and Wrestling* cartoon show?
A. Junkyard Dog
B. Wendi Richter
C. Freddie Blassie
D. Jimmy Snuka

58. True or False: Pedro Morales defeated Stan Stasiak to win his first WWF World title.

59. True or False: Adrian Adonis and Jesse Ventura held the WWF World tag team title.

60. True or False: Starrcade 1987 was WCW's first pay-per-view.

61. True or False: Jake Roberts was a member of Paul Ellering's Legion of Doom.

62. True or False: Jim Brunzell and Greg Gagne lost their second AWA World tag team title to Sheik Adnan El Kaissey and Jerry Blackwell.

63. True or False: Wendi Richter was the reigning WWF Women's champion going into the first Wrestlemania.

64. True or False: Hulk Hogan is a former IWGP heavyweight champion.

65. True or False: During a *20/20* report. Dr. David Schultz assaulted Geraldo Rivera for saying that wrestling was fake.

66. Out of Nick Bockwinkel's four reigns as AWA World champion, how many titles were won in the ring?
    A. Four
    B. Three
    C. Two
    D. One

67. Who defeated The Road Warriors for the AWA World tag team title?
    A. The Fabulous Freebirds
    B. Jimmy Garvin and Steve Regal
    C. Baron Von Raschke and The Crusher
    D. Ken Patera and Jerry Blackwell

68. Who was the first recognized AWA World champion?
    A. Verne Gagne
    B. Gene Kiniski
    C. Pat O'Connor
    D. Dick Hutton

69. Who did Rick Martel defeat to become AWA World champion?
    A. Jumbo Tsuruta
    B. Nick Bockwinkel
    C. Stan Hansen
    D. Otto Wanz

70. Who was the second-to-the-last AWA champion?
    A. Mr. Saito

B. Larry Zbyszko
C. Jerry Lawler
D. Curt Hennig

71. Who did Ric Flair defeat for his first NWA World title in 1981?
    A. Harley Race
    B. Dory Funk
    C. Dusty Rhodes
    D. Tommy Rich

72. What type of match did Roddy Piper and Greg Valentine wrestle in at Starrcade 1983?
    A. Death Match
    B. First Blood Match
    C. Cage Match
    D. Dog Collar Match

73. True or False: Boris Malenko, father of Dean Malenko, is a former AWA World tag team champion.

74. True or False: Jesse "The Body" Ventura once wrestled as "Mr. V."

75. True or False: The Original Midnight Express were contenders, but never held the AWA World tag team title.

76. What was the name of the group competition conducted in the final year of the AWA's existence?
    A. The Team Challenge Series
    B. King of the Hill
    C. Winner Takes All
    D. Round Robin

77. When Super Destroyer Mark II fired Lord Alfred Hayes, who did he select to be his manager?
    A. Bobby "The Brain" Heenan
    B. Freddie Blassie
    C. Jimmy Hart
    D. Captain Lou Albano

78. Super Destroyer Mark II would wrestle under what famous name later on in his career?
    A. King Kong Bundy

B. Jimmy "Superfly" Snuka
C. Sergeant Slaughter
D. Super Dog Mark

79. True or False: AWA promoter Wally Karbo promised "fines and suspensions."

80. Bobby Heenan ignited a feud by breaking the radio of what AWA star?
A. Adrian Adonis
B. Ricky "The Dragon" Steamboat
C. "Mr. Wonderful" Paul Orndorff
D. Buck "Rock and Roll" Zumhofe

81. What was Adrian Adonis' nickname in the AWA?
A. Goldilocks
B. Golden Boy
C. Golden God
D. Goldfinger

82. What was the name of Goldberg's autobiography?
A. *I'm Next*
B. *It's Good To Be Goldberg*
C. *Golden Opportunity*
D. *The Best*

83. What was the name of the poetic broadcast partner of Joey Styles who called himself the "Quintessential Stud Muffin"?
A. Jerry Lawler
B. Bobby Heenan
C. Joel Gertner
D. Mean Gene Okerlund

84. What organization did Stevie Richards and The Blue Meanie form in ECW?
A. The Stevie Meanies
B. Blue Velvet
C. The Blue Man Group
D. The Blue World Order

85. What was the actual name of the ECW Arena?
    A. Viking Hall
    B. St. Catherine's Gymnasium
    C. Mustang Auditorium
    D. Main Street Arena

86. What did ECW Arena double as on non-wrestling nights?
    A. Casino
    B. Bingo hall
    C. Basketball gym
    D. Reception hall

87. What three wrestlers were primarily featured in "Beyond The Mat"?
    A. Stone Cold Steve Austin, Mankind and Bret Hart
    B. Goldberg, Terry Funk and Triple H
    C. Mankind, Jake Roberts, and Terry Funk
    D. The Rock, Scott Hall and Jake Roberts

INTERNATIONAL

Just like North America itself, professional wrestling has received significant contributions from immigrants and wrestling organizations within various foreign countries. If not for the wrestling circuits in Europe, Asia and Mexico, many of professional wrestling's biggest stars might not have developed the moves and personas which brought them fame and fortune in the large federations during the 1980s, 90s and beyond.

The wrestlers of today owe a debt of gratitude to people like Andre the Giant, Hulk Hogan and Antonio Inoki (and countless others before them), who worked their way through small venues in faraway places within Europe and Japan before making their mark in the United States.

Wrestling in its original form, the Greco-Roman style, is said to date back to the Roman Empire, and maybe back to the Egyptians. But it wasn't until German and Irish immigrants brought wrestling over to the "New World" in the post-Civil War era that the Americanized version began showing up at carnivals and county fairs.

This new sport was popular among immigrants, who used it as a way to make a living despite prejudices and language barriers.

Wrestling is not just a sport that came to America. It still experiences great popularity in other countries today. Japan and Mexico boast some of the richest wrestling traditions around, with Japanese stars like Antonio Inoki, The Giant Baba, and Jumbo Tsuruta and Mexican grapplers including Tito Santana, Mil Mascaras and Rey Misterio, Jr.

Beyond these current hotbeds of international wrestling, today's biggest federations have seen an influx of international wrestlers over the years, though some only *claim* to be from foreign lands:

England: The British Bulldog, Axl Rotten, Lord Steve Regal, David Finlay, "The Belfast Bruiser."

Germany: Fritz Von Erich, Hans Schmidt, Berlyn, Kurt Von Hess, The Hun, Fredrick Von Schacht, "The Milwaukee Murder Master."

Russia (former U.S.S.R.): Ivan Koloff, Nikolai Volkoff, Nikita Koloff, Boris Dragoff.

Within this chapter you'll find great trivia about professional wrestling's foreign superstars, and you might even get a sense of the rich heritage wrestling has within the cultures of many other countries outside of North America.

1. What country are The Bushwhackers billed from?
   A. Australia
   B. New Zealand
   C. England
   D. Scotland

2. Tito Santana, a native of Tocula, Mexico, won the WWF Intercontinental title in 1984. What other name and gimmick did he wrestle under in the early 1990s?
   A. El Toro
   B. El Loco
   C. El Matador
   D. El Vaca

3. Which wrestler did Muhammad Ali face in 1976?
   A. Antonio Inoki
   B. Gorilla Monsoon
   C. Jesse "The Body" Ventura
   D. "Superstar" Billy Graham

4. Which Japanese wrestler defeated Bob Buckland in 1979, interrupting his five-year hold on the WWF title, and also beat Hulk Hogan in 1984?
   A. Jumbo Osaki
   B. Antonio Inoki
   C. The Tokyo Terror
   D. Godzilla

5. Jesse Ventura is not the only wrestler to turn to politics. Which international grappler was elected to his country's parliament?
   A. Lord Alfred Hayes
   B. Jerry "The King" Lawler
   C. The British Bulldog
   D. Antonio Inoki

6. In the late 1960s and early 1970s, Madison Square Garden banned masked wrestlers, but the popularity of one such wrestler caused MSG to lift its ban in 1972. Who was the first masked wrestler to appear in Madison Square Garden?
   A. Ricky "The Dragon" Steamboat
   B. Tito Santana
   C. Rey Misterio, Jr.
   D. Mil Mascaras

7. Mexican mighty-mite Rey Misterio, Jr. stands 5' 3" and tips the scales at only 140 pounds, but which two giant-sized opponents has he defeated?
   A. Paul Wight and The Undertaker
   B. Kane and The Undertaker
   C. Kevin Nash and Bam Bam Bigelow
   D. Kane and Kevin Nash

8. Who won more titles than any wrestler in the history of Japanese wrestling?
   A. The Giant Baba
   B. Antonio Inoki
   C. Tajiri
   D. Masato Tanaka

9. Which wrestler's character claiming to be from England is also known as "The King of the Foreign Objects Matches"?
   A. The British Bulldog
   B. Axl Rotten
   C. Abdullah the Butcher
   D. Lord Alfred Hayes

10. What is the name of the type of high-flying freestyle wrestling seen in Mexico?
    A. Mas Alta
    B. En Fuego
    C. Los Locos
    D. Lucha Libre

11. Who was the first Asian wrestler to win a version of the world heavyweight title?
    A. Tojo Yammamoto
    B. Gobar Goho
    C. Giant Baba
    D. Antonio Inoki

12. How many masks did Mil Mascaras claim to have?
    A. One hundred
    B. One million
    C. Ten
    D. One thousand

13. Who were the first PWF tag team champions?
    A. The Road Warriors
    B. Bruiser Brody and Stan Hansen
    C. Jumbo Tsuruta and Genichiro Tenryu
    D. Riki Chosu and Masa Saito

14. Who did Big Van Vader defeat in his December 27, 1987 debut?
    A. Riki Chosu
    B. Antonio Inoki
    C. Giant Baba
    D. Hiroshi Hasse

15. True or False: Chris Benoit wrestled in Japan under a mask as Black Tiger.

16. Who was the first Triple Crown champion?
    A. Stan Hansen
    B. Jumbo Tsuruta
    C. Giant Baba
    D. Antonio Inoki

17. Who did Jushin "Thunder" Liger defeat for his first IWGP junior heavy-weight title?
    A. Great Muta
    B. Riki Chosu
    C. Chris Benoit
    D. Shiro Koshinaka

18. How did the 1995 feud between Mascara Ano Dos Mil and Perro Aguayo start?
    A. Chair to Aguayo's head
    B. Brass knuckles to Aguayo's head
    C. Beer bottle to Aguayo's head
    D. Ring bell to Aguayo's head

19. What wrestling organization was not a part of the 1996 World Peace Festival in Los Angeles?
    A. New Japan
    B. EMLL
    C. WCW
    D. WWF

20. In response to Keiji Muto's "Great Muta" gimmick, Atsushi Onita came up with one of his own. What was his 1999 mocking persona?
    A. The Great Muto
    B. The Great Nita
    C. The Great Sushi
    D. The Great Keiji

21. True or False: Antonio Inoki holds a victory over Andre the Giant.

22. True or False: Mitsuharu Misawa was the second Tiger Mask.

23. True or False: Hiroshi Hase lost in his bid to become a member of the Japanese House of Councilors.

24. What Japanese tag team wrestled Demolition at Wrestlemania 7?
    A. Jumbo Tsuruta and Giant Baba
    B. Giant Baba and Genichiro Tenryu
    C. Antonio Inoki and Koji Kitao
    D. Koji Kitao and Genichiro Tenryu

THE NAME GAME

The things that stand out about wrestlers and professional wrestling during its long, bizarre history are names. Nothing else in the history of sports or sports entertainment has given us so many incredibly unusual, funny, original names.

Sure, there are a few good names throughout the sports world. In pro football there was "Mean" Joe Green, Randy "The Manster" White, Jack Lambert, also called "Count Dracula in Cleats," Night Train Lane; in pro basketball there was Air Jordan, Magic Johnson, Dr. Dunkenstein, The Iceman, The Mailman, The Human Highlight Film and The Answer; major league baseball had Dennis "Oil Can" Boyd, "Charlie Hustle" Pete Rose, "Shoeless" Joe Jackson, and "The Sultan of Swat" Babe Ruth; pro hockey boasts "The Golden Jet" Bobby Hull, "Mr. Hockey" Gordie Howe, and "The Great One" Wayne Gretzky; and, of course, boxing has its share of unusual monikers: Iron Mike Tyson, Evander "The Real Deal" Holyfield, Bonecrusher Smith, Tommy "The Hitman" Hearns, "Hands of Stone" Roberto Duran, and "The Greatest" Muhammad Ali.

But, if you consider all the great names of all five of these sports, you'd still fall short of the outrageous names and titles wrestlers have given themselves. Here are just a few: The Crusher, The Bruiser, Killer Kowalski, Iron Sheik, Big John Studd, Andre the Giant, The Junkyard Dog, Bam Bam Bigelow, The Undertaker, Kane, Hulk Hogan, Goldberg and The Rock.

But more than that, wrestlers are notorious for changing names and alternating gimmicks at the drop of a hat, all in the name of giving the fans what they want and developing a popular persona.

Did you know that before Kane was Kane, he took the name of The New Diesel after Kevin Nash (then known as Diesel) left the WWF for the WCW? Or how about X-Pac? He was known as The Lightning Kid, The Cannonball Kid and The Kamikaze Kid before he settled on X-Pac in the WWF in the late 1990s.

This chapter explores these types of name changes with great trivia questions you can use to stump your friends. But also inside, we reveal the real names of the men who play your favorite professional wrestling characters. Sure, everyone knows Goldberg's actual name is Bill Goldberg, and we all know that Hulk Hogan's name is actually Terry Bollea, but through our trivia questions we reveal the real names of wrestlers like Sid Vicious, The Ultimate Warrior, Rob Van Dam, Sean Michaels and Kane. Want to know who's who? Read on!

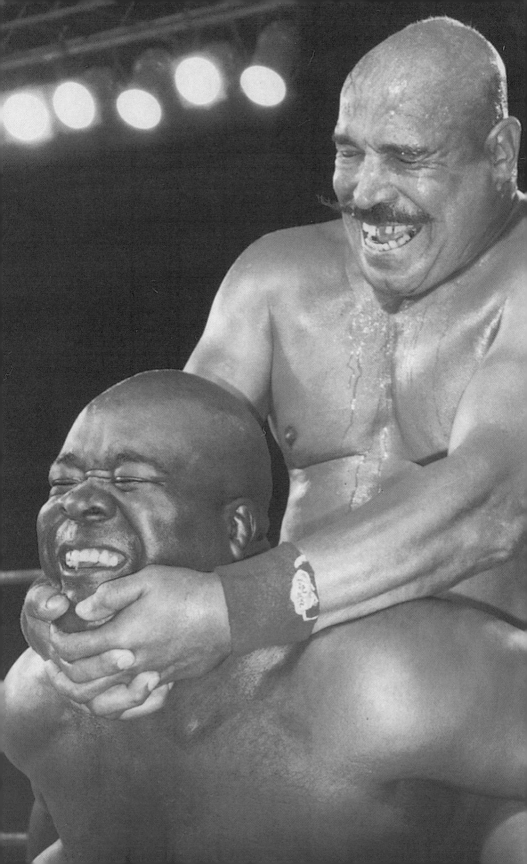

1. What were the names of The Bushwhackers?
    A. Bo and Luke
    B. Luke and Butch
    C. Kyle and Earl
    D. Spike and Mike

2. What name did The Bushwhackers go by before they were The Bushwhackers?
    A. The Good Ol' Boys
    B. The Rangers
    C. The Rednecks
    D. The Sheepherders

3. Which wrestler's real name is Michael Hickenbottom?
    A. King Kong Bundy
    B. Raven
    C. Shawn Michaels
    D. Spike Dudley

4. Which wrestler's real name is Terry Brunk?
    A. The Iron Sheik
    B. Sabu
    C. The Junkyard Dog
    D. Big Boss Man

5. Which wrestler's real name is Monte Sopp?
    A. Balls Mahoney
    B. Diamond Dallas Page
    C. Ric Flair
    D. Billy Gunn

6. Which wrestler's real name is James Reihel?
    A. Jimmy "Superfly" Snuka
    B. Dean Malenko
    C. Kane
    D. Rowdy Roddy Piper

7. Which wrestler's real name is Larry Pfohl?
    A. Lex Luger
    B. Randy Savage
    C. Chris Jericho
    D. Justin Credible

8. Which wrestler's real name is Roderick Toombs?
   A. Bam Bam Bigelow
   B. Billy Kidman
   C. Rowdy Roddy Piper
   D. The Undertaker

9. Which wrestler's real name is Robert Szatowski?
   A. Triple H
   B. Road Dogg
   C. Jake "The Snake" Roberts
   D. Rob Van Dam

10. Which wrestler's real name is Ed Farhat?
    A. Tazz
    B. The Sheik (1960s-70s)
    C. The Iron Sheik (1970s-80s)
    D. Rikishi

11. Which wrestler's real name is Jim Hellwig?
    A. The Ultimate Warrior
    B. Sting
    C. Sgt. Slaughter
    D. Perry Saturn

12. Which wrestler's real name is Page Falkenburg?
    A. Psicosis
    B. Bruiser Brody
    C. Diamond Dallas Page
    D. Ricky "The Dragon" Steamboat

13. The Ultimate Warrior was known by a similar name earlier in his career. What was it?
    A. The Ultimate Man
    B. The Wonderful Warrior
    C. The Dingo Warrior
    D. The Monster Warrior

14. Today, everyone knows The Rock. But in the 1980s another wrestler was known as The Rock. What name was the original The Rock better known by?
    A. Rocky Bullwinkle
    B. Hulk Hogan
    C. Antonio Rocca

D. The Ultimate Warrior

15. Which wrestler's real name is Glenn Jacobs?
   A. Billy Gunn
   B. Kane
   C. Goldberg
   D. The Undertaker

16. What other ugly character was Kane known as?
   A. Mankind
   B. Sid Vicious
   C. Isaac Yankem
   D. Gangrel

17. Which of the following character names was NOT used by Mick Foley?
   A. Cactus Jack
   B. Mankind
   C. Dude Love
   D. The Cajun Sensation
   E. They were all used by Mick Foley

18. Which of the following character names was NOT used by Glenn Jacobs?
   A. Kane
   B. The Christmas Creature
   C. Unabom
   D. Isaac Yankem
   E. The New Diesel
   F. They were all used by Glenn Jacobs

19. Which of the following character names was NOT used by Sean Waltman?
   A. The Lightning Kid
   B. The Kamikaze Kid
   C. The Cannonball Kid
   D. The Dynamite Kid
   E. The 1-2-3 Kid
   F. Syxx
   G. X-Pac
   H. They were all used by Sean Waltman

20. Brutus Beefcake was also known as Brutus the Barber. Which of the following names did he also go by?

A. The Booty Man
B. Zodiac
C. The Disciple
D. A and B
E. A and C
F. B and C
G. A, B and C

21. True or False: Stone Cold Steve Austin was once known as The RingMaster.

22. True or False: Stone Cold Steve Austin was once part of the tag team duo called The Hollywood Blonds.

23. "The Macho Man" Randy Savage has wrestled under one or both of these names for almost 25 years. Which of the following other character names did he NOT use?
A. The Spider
B. The Executioner
C. The Destroyer
D. The Killer

24. Which wrestler once held the persona "The Narcissist"?
A. Mr. Wonderful
B. The Ultimate Warrior
C. Lex Luger
D. Shawn Michaels

25. Which of the following names has Kevin Nash NOT used inside the ring?
A. Steel
B. Iron Man
C. Diesel
D. Oz
E. Vinnie Vegas

26. Which of the following names has Scott Hall NOT used inside the ring?
A. Starship Coyote
B. Diamond Studd
C. The Greaser
D. Razor Ramon

27. Which wrestler started out with the name Terra Ryzing?
    A. Triple H
    B. The Rock
    C. Rob Van Dam
    D. X-Pac

28. What is Sid Vicious' real name?
    A. Sid Valentine
    B. Sam Johnson
    C. Johnny Rotten
    D. Sid Eudy

29. Rikishi was also known as what masked wrestler in 1997?
    A. The Super Sheik
    B. The Sultan
    C. Kane
    D. Tiger Mask

30. Steve Lombardi played which of the following characters in the WWF?
    A. Abe "Knuckleball" Schwartz
    B. The MVP
    C. The Brooklyn Brawler
    D. All of the above

31. Who was Scott Hall in WCW before jumping to the WWF as Razor Ramon in 1992?
    A. The Diamond Studd
    B. The Bad Guy
    C. The Diamond Cutter
    D. The Toothpick Guy

32. Who did Barry Windham turn on in 1988 to join the Four Horsemen?
    A. Mike Rotundo
    B. Lex Luger
    C. Dustin Rhodes
    D. Blackjack Mulligan

33. Brad Armstrong did NOT portray one of the following:
    A. Arachnaman
    B. The Candyman
    C. Black Blood
    D. Fantasia

31

WCW

These days professional wrestling is a three-headed monster. One head is the World Wrestling Federation (WWF), one head is all of the other small "indie" organizations, and the third head, of course, is World Championship Wrestling (WCW).

True wrestling fans often can't get enough of their favorite blood sport, so following the stars and plotlines from both the WWF and WCW is a must. The WCW has a long, star-studded history, one that compares favorably to that of the WWF.

The WCW could also be called the wrestling organization formerly known as the NWA (National Wrestling Alliance). The NWA has been around since 1948, but due to the dominance of the WWF (especially on television), the NWA all but folded until Ted Turner bought it in the early 1980s. But, Turner did not have the rights to the name or initials NWA. So, what was the NWA became Turner's WCW, which was already the name of Turner's hit Saturday night show on his superstation, TBS.

Thus began the war between Ted Turner and Vince McMahon, Jr. Ted Turner vowed to prevent the WWF from monopolizing wrestling on cable television, and he did so with his own wrestling federation on his own cable network. The reason for the hatred between the two? There are all sorts of rumors on this subject, but the two that seem to receive the most attention are that Turner was upset with McMahon, Jr.'s demand for prime time slots, or that he was mad with McMahon for trying to buy the NWA's wrestling talent away from then owner Jim Crockett, which would effectively cut the legs out from under the struggling NWA, giving the WWF a monopoly.

Whatever the case, the rest is history as the feud and competition between the WCW and WWF resulted in the craziest plotlines, highest television ratings, highest attendance records and most pay-per-view viewers in the history of the sport. The rise of the WCW in the 1980s and 90s to battle the WWF played a major part in wrestling becoming the sports entertainment juggernaught it is today.

But what is the main reason the WCW has had so much success? The wrestlers. The characters and gimmicks that the athletes within the WCW have come up with are among the most outrageous and captivating in wrestling history. Wrestlers like Diamond Dallas Page, Rey Misterio, Jr., Buff Bagwell, Hulk Hogan, and of course, Goldberg have given the WCW a firm foothold among wrestling fans and has solidified its place in pro wrestling history.

In this chapter you'll find some great trivia questions about your favorite WCW stars and most memorable matches from the WWF's most hated and feared rival.

1. Many celebrities have entered the ring over the years, but only one has ever won a belt. Which celebrity won a world championship belt in a tag team match?
   A. David Arquette
   B. Mr. T
   C. Dennis Rodman
   D. Jay Leno

2. Who was WCW Rookie of the Year in 1997?
   A. Rey Misterio, Jr.
   B. Goldberg
   C. Prince Iaukea
   D. The Giant

3. How many times has Rey Misterio, Jr. won the WCW cruiserweight title?
   A. 3 times
   B. 4 times
   C. 5 times
   D. 7 times

4. How many times did the tag team duo known as Harlem Heat, consisting of Booker T and Stevie Ray, win the WCW tag team title from 1994 to 1997?
   A. 8 times
   B. 10 times
   C. 6 times
   D. 12 times

5. Who did Booker T defeat to win the WCW World Title in July 2000?
   A. Chris Jericho
   B. Billy Kidman
   C. Goldberg
   D. Jeff Jarrett

6. How many times has Hulk Hogan won the WCW World Title?
   A. 5
   B. 4
   C. 6
   D. 0

7. Which wrestler is also known as "The Man of a Thousand Holds"?
   A. Mil Mascaras
   B. Dean Malenko
   C. X-Pac
   D. Billy Gunn

8. Which wrestler's finishing moves are called The Nail in the Coffin and The Vampire Spike?
   A. Vampiro
   B. Kane
   C. The Undertaker
   D. Gangrel

9. What college did Goldberg attend to play football?
   A. Penn State
   B. Boston College
   C. University of Virginia
   D. University of Georgia

10. What position did he play?
    A. Defensive tackle
    B. Noseguard
    C. Linebacker
    D. Defensive end

11. Who was Goldberg's opponent in his first-ever WCW match?
    A. Tazz
    B. Hugh Morrus
    C. The Giant
    D. Rikishi

12. When "Big Show" Paul Wight debuted in the WCW in 1995, what legendary wrestler was said to be his father?
    A. Bruno Sammartino
    B. Gorilla Monsoon
    C. Andre the Giant
    D. Haystacks Calhoun

13. Which wrestler actually worked as a male dancer prior to his career in wrestling?
    A. Buff Bagwell
    B. Val Venis
    C. Triple H
    D. Sean Michaels

14. What is the name of Buff Bagwell's finishing move?
    A. The Big LeBuffski
    B. The Buff Blockbuster
    C. The Buffinator
    D. Buff the Magic Dragon

15. Which four WCW defectees are known in the WWF as The Radicalz?
    A. Chris Benoit
    B. Perry Saturn
    C. Eddy Guerrero
    D. Dean Malenko
    E. Paul Wight
    F. Tazz

16. What was The Sandman's name in WCW?
    A. Hak
    B. King Extreme
    C. Bud
    D. The Sandman

17. Who did Bill Goldberg challenge in a February 1999 episode of *The Tonight Show*?
    A. Bret Hart
    B. Hulk Hogan
    C. Steve Austin
    D. Gillberg

18. True or False: The Godfather also portrayed the mystical Papa Shango.

19. True or False: Upon joining the WWF, Bill Irwin played a plumber named T.L. Hopper.

20. Which two men battled for the NWA heavyweight championship belt at The Great American Bash 1990?
    A. Ric Flair
    B. Big Van Vader

C. Sting
D. "Mean" Mark Callous
E. Harley Race
F. Lex Luger

21. Who were the last two to enter the War Games at 1992 Wrestle War?
    A. Dustin Rhodes
    B. Larry Zbyszko
    C. Rick Rude
    D. Bobby Eaton
    E. Nikita Koloff
    F. Ricky Steamboat
    G. Arn Anderson
    H. Sting

22. Who won the WCW heavyweight championship match at Superbrawl X?
    A. Scott Hall
    B. Jeff Jarrett
    C. Sid Vicious
    D. Ric Flair

23. Which of these matches took place at Clash of the Champions XVI in 1991?
    A. Ron Simmons vs. Rick Rude
    B. Lex Luger vs. Sid Vicious
    C. Lex Luger vs. Badstreet
    D. Sid Vicious vs. Joey Maggs

24. Who successfully defended the WCW championship at Halloween Havoc 1991?
    A. Sting
    B. Lex Luger
    C. Ron Simmons
    D. Ravishing Rick Rude
    E. Ric Flair

25. Who successfully defended the WCW heavyweight championship at Superbrawl VII?
    A. The Giant
    B. Eddy Guerrero
    C. Rowdy Roddy Piper
    D. Kevin Sullivan
    E. Hulk Hogan
    F. Chris Jericho

26. Who contended in the Death Match at Halloween Havoc 1997?
    A. Hulk Hogan
    B. Diamond Dallas Page
    C. Roddy Piper
    D. Scott Hall
    E. Lex Luger
    F. Randy Savage

27. Who were on the winning side in the six-man Lucha Libre match at Bash at the Beach 1997?
    A. Hector Garza
    B. Lizmark, Jr.
    C. Villano IV
    D. Juventud Guerrera
    E. Psicosis
    F. La Parka

28. How many matches at Halloween Havoc 1997 ended by submission?
    A. One
    B. Four
    C. Three
    D. None
    E. Two
    F. Five

29. What was the result of the tag team championship match at Clash of the Champions XIV?
    A. Sting & Lex Luger were disqualified
    B. Doom left the arena and were counted out
    C. No decision, because of outside interference
    D. Doom (the reigning champions) won
    E. Sting & Lex Luger won

30. At the War Games at Fall Brawl 1993, who were the two men to enter the steel cage first?
    A. Vader
    B. Shockmaster
    C. Sting
    D. Harlem Heat Kane
    E. Davey Boy Smith
    F. Harlem Heat Koal
    G. Dustin Rhodes
    H. Sid Vicious

31. At the WCW/New Japan Tokyo Dome Supershow in 1996, which two
    men competed for the IWGP title?
    A. Tatsumi Fujinami
    B. Shinya Hashimoto
    C. Tenryu
    D. Nobuhiko Takada

32. Who did Ric Flair defeat at Starrcade 1984?
    A. Ricky Steamboat
    B. Wahoo McDaniel
    C. Dusty Rhodes
    D. Harley Race

33. What was the result of the 30-minute Iron Man for the US
    championship at Beach Blast 1993?
    A. Dustin Rhodes won the belt with two falls to one
    B. Rick Rude won the belt with four falls to one
    C. Dustin Rhodes won the belt with one fall to none
    D. The match was a draw
    E. Rick Rude won the belt with three falls to two

34. What was the decision in the heavyweight championship match at the
    1994 Spring Stampede?
    A. Ric Flair was awarded the decision after a simultaneous pincount
    B. Ric Flair won the match by disqualification
    C. Ricky "The Dragon" Steamboat was awarded the decision after a
       simultaneous pincount
    D. Ricky "The Dragon" Steamboat won the match on a pinfall
    E. Ric Flair won the match on a pinfall
    F. The title was vacated after a simultaneous pincount

35. At the third Superbrawl in 1993, who successfully defended the WCW
    championship?
    A. Barry Windham
    B. Dustin Rhodes
    C. Sting
    D. Maxx Payne
    E. The Great Muta
    F. Vader

36. Who successfully defended the WCW heavyweight championship at Superbrawl IX?
   A. Ric Flair
   B. "Hollywood" Hulk Hogan
   C. Scott Hall
   D. Kevin Nash
   E. Diamond Dallas Page

37. At Superbrawl II, who became the WCW heavyweight champion?
   A. Rick Rude
   B. Ricky Steamboat
   C. Jushin Thunder Liger
   D. Brian Pillman
   E. Steve Austin
   F. Lex Luger
   G. Sting

38. Who won the WCW heavyweight championship at Slamboree 1999?
   A. Hollywood Hogan
   B. Goldberg
   C. Ric Flair
   D. Sting
   E. Kevin Nash

39. What was so special about the Buff Bagwell vs. Rowdy Roddy Piper match at Bash at the Beach 1999?
   A. It was a steel cage match
   B. It was a 10 round boxing match
   C. It was a 30-minute Iron Man match
   D. It was a three out of four falls match

40. At Superbrawl VI, who won the WCW heavyweight championship?
   A. Diamond Dallas Page
   B. Ric Flair
   C. One Man Gang
   D. Johnny B. Badd
   E. Konnan
   F. Macho Man
   G. The Giant
   H. Hulk Hogan

41. Which teams competed in the tag team championship match at Superbrawl X?

A. David Flair & Crowbar
B. Wolfpac
C. The Mamalukes
D. Kronic
E. Harlem Heat

42. Who successfully defended the WCW TV championship at Fall Brawl 1999?
A. Hulk Hogan
B. Rick Steiner
C. Sting
D. Sid Vicious
E. Perry Saturn
F. Chris Benoit
G. Goldberg

43. Who won the Battle Bowl final at Slamboree 1996?
A. Rocko Rock
B. Earl Robert Eaton
C. Dirty Dick Slater
D. Diamond Dallas Page
E. Scott Norton
F. Johnny Grunge
G. Ice Train
H. Barbarian

44. Who won the inaugural and only Bunkhouse Stampede pay-per-view in January of 1988?
A. The Barbarian
B. Nikita Koloff
C. The Road Warriors
D. Dusty Rhodes

45. Who was the last man to hold the NWA Western States Heritage title?
A. Barry Windham
B. Dusty Rhodes
C. Larry Zbyszko
D. Arn Anderson

46. What mysterious masked wrestler who claimed to be from Sting's past feuded with the then-WCW World champion in 1990?
A. The Black Scorpion
B. The Yellow Dog

C. The Midnight Rider
D. Blackblood

47. Who was Doom's original manager?
    A. Woman
    B. Diamond Dallas Page
    C. Teddy Long
    D. Michael Hayes

48. Who was the special guest referee in the Halloween Havoc 1989 main event of Ric Flair and Sting versus Terry Funk and The Great Muta?
    A. Ole Anderson
    B. Lou Thesz
    C. Pat O'Connor
    D. Bruno Sammartino

49. What was the name of the final WCW pay-per-view under Time Warner ownership?
    A. Greed
    B. Sin
    C. Superbrawl Revenge
    D. Spring Stampede

50. What was the final title created by WCW under Time Warner ownership?
    A. Cruiserweight title
    B. Hardcore title
    C. Hardcore tag team title
    D. Cruiserweight tag team title

51. Who was forced to retire because of a match stipulation at SuperBrawl Revenge in February of 2001?
    A. Ric Flair
    B. Goldberg
    C. Kevin Nash
    D. Diamond Dallas Page

52. What was the first prime time wrestling special on WTBS?
    A. Clash of the Champions
    B. Superstars On The Superstation
    C. The Crockett Cup
    D. Fall Brawl

53. Who won the first-ever Jim Crockett, Sr. Memorial Cup tag team tournament?
    A. The Road Warriors
    B. Arn Anderson and Tully Blanchard
    C. Sting and Lex Luger
    D. Dusty Rhodes and Nikita Koloff

54. Who was not an original member of the Four Horsemen?
    A. Tully Blanchard
    B. Barry Windham
    C. Arn Anderson
    D. Ole Anderson

55. Who did Dusty Rhodes and Nikita Koloff defeat for the second Crockett Cup in April of 1987?
    A. Ivan Koloff and Don Kernodle
    B. Arn Anderson and Ric Flair
    C. The Road Warriors
    D. Tully Blanchard and Lex Luger

56. What city hosted the first Clash of the Champions?
    A. Atlanta, Georgia
    B. Charleston, South Carolina
    C. Greensboro, North Carolina
    D. New Orleans, Louisiana

57. What was the first title that Lex Luger held?
    A. Florida heavyweight championship
    B. North American heavyweight championship
    C. Southern heavyweight championship
    D. Mid-South heavyweight championship

58. Who did Lex Luger defeat for his first championship?
    A. Wahoo McDaniel
    B. Mike Graham
    C. Tully Blanchard
    D. Sir Oliver Humperdink

59. Which pay-per-view featured the return of Ric Flair to WCW in 1993?
    A. SuperBrawl
    B. Starrcade
    C. The Great American Bash
    D. Slamboree

60. Who received 20 stab wounds during a 1993 brawl with Sid Vicious in Blackburn, England?
A. Big Van Vader
B. Paul Orndorff
C. Arn Anderson
D. Ric Flair

61. What other former WWF star debuted when The Road Warriors returned at the Clash of the Champions on January 23, 1996?
A. Randy Savage
B. Elizabeth
C. The Steiners
D. Brutus Beefcake

62. On what holiday did Scott Hall make his WCW debut in 1996?
A. Memorial Day
B. Labor Day
C. Independence Day
D. Easter Monday

63. What longtime foe confronted Hulk Hogan after his Halloween Havoc 1996 match?
A. Randy Savage
B. Roddy Piper
C. Jimmy Hart
D. Bret Hart

64. What was the NWO "Fake Sting's" former persona?
A. Glacier
B. Mortis
C. Buddy Lee Parker
D. Cobra

65. Who was the first member of WCW to join the New World Order?
A. Sting
B. Eric Bischoff
C. The Giant
D. Buff Bagwell

66. Who did Dennis Rodman and Hulk Hogan lose to in Rodman's wrestling debut in July 1997?
A. Lex Luger and The Giant
B. Lex Luger and Sting

C. Diamond Dallas Page and Jay Leno
D. Diamond Dallas Page and Karl Malone

67. Who did Diamond Dallas Page pin to win his first WCW World title?
A. Hulk Hogan
B. Randy Savage
C. Sting
D. Ric Flair

68. To start his brief 1999 heel run, who did Sting turn on at Fall Brawl?
A. Hulk Hogan
B. Lex Luger
C. Rick Steiner
D. The Giant

69. What reigning ECW World champion made his WCW debut in April 2000?
A. Raven
B. Mike Awesome
C. Shane Douglas
D. Bam Bam Bigelow

70. Starrcade 1989 was dubbed "The Night of the" what?
A. Iron Man
B. Stinger
C. Nature Boy
D. Ultimate Revenge

71. Who replaced Eric Bischoff as the administrative head of WCW following Bischoff's ouster in September of 1999?
A. Bill Busch
B. Vince Russo
C. Kevin Sullivan
D. Terry Taylor

72. Who did Bret Hart wrestle in a tribute match to his brother on October 4, 1999?
A. Dean Malenko
B. Chris Benoit
C. Chris Jericho
D. Lance Storm

73. Who did Bret Hart wrestle in his first WCW match following the death of his brother Owen?
    A. Ric Flair
    B. Bill Goldberg
    C. Hulk Hogan
    D. Kevin Nash

74. Who won the NWA World tag team title at the first Clash of the Champions?
    A. Arn Anderson and Tully Blanchard
    B. Lex Luger and Barry Windham
    C. The Road Warriors
    D. The Midnight Express

75. What were WWF's Bushwhackers known as in the NWA?
    A. The Kiwi Men
    B. The New Zealand Militia
    C. The Sheepherders
    D. The Bushwhackers

76. Who beat The Road Warriors for the NWA World tag team title at Clash of the Champions 6 in April 1989?
    A. Mike Rotundo and Steve Williams
    B. Kevin Sullivan and Danny Spivey
    C. Mike Rotundo and Kevin Sullivan
    D. Steve Williams and Danny Spivey

77. What did The Dynamic Dudes (Shane Douglas and Johnny Ace) throw into the crowds?
    A. Pants
    B. Bandanas
    C. Sunglasses
    D. Frisbees

78. What bell-ringing tag team made their debut at the Clash of the Champions 7 in July 1989?
    A. The Ding-A-Lings
    B. The Ding Dongs
    C. The Bellhops
    D. The Bellboys

79. Who has enjoyed the most reigns as WCW World Television
    champion?
    A. Booker T
    B. Steven/William Regal
    C. Arn Anderson
    D. Steve Austin

80. Who was the first WCW Cruiserweight champion?
    A. Dean Malenko
    B. Chris Benoit
    C. Shinjiro Ohtani
    D. Rey Misterio, Jr.

81. Who won the 1991 tournament to crown WCW World six-man tag
    team
    champions?
    A. Dutch Mantel, Buddy Landell, and Dr. X
    B. Dustin Rhodes, Tom Zenk, and Big Josh
    C. The York Foundation
    D. Tommy Rich, Ricky Morton, and The Junkyard Dog

82. Who were the last reigning WCW United States tag team champions?
    A. Ron Simmons and Big Josh
    B. Dick Slater and The Barbarian
    C. Greg Valentine and The Taylor-Made Man (Terry Taylor)
    D. The Fabulous Freebirds

83. How did Randy Savage win his first WCW World title in November
    1995?
    A. Battle Royal
    B. Tournament Final
    C. Commissioner's Decree
    D. Four-Way Match

84. Who was the first WCW Hardcore champion?
    A. Brian Knobs
    B. Norman Smiley
    C. Bam Bam Bigelow
    D. Terry Funk

85. Who won the most WCW Hardcore championships?
    A. Norman Smiley
    B. Fit Finlay

C. Terry Funk
D. Brian Knobs

86. True or False: When WCW World champion Ric Flair left WCW in 1991, he was also stripped of the NWA World title.

87. True or False: Hulk Hogan signed with WCW in 1993.

88. True or False: Hulk Hogan pushed The Giant off the roof of Cobo Hall at Halloween Havoc 1995.

89. True or False: The Iron Sheik once challenged Sting for the WCW Television title.

90. True or False: At Halloween Havoc 1995, Jimmy Hart turned on The Giant to reunite with Hulk Hogan.

91. True or False: Hulk Hogan defeated Roddy Piper in their Starrcade 1996 match.

92. True or False: Bret Hart made his WCW pay-per-view debut as a referee.

93. True or False: Chris Benoit and Dean Malenko never held the WCW World tag team title.

94. True or False: During his run in WCW, Cactus Jack never received a world title shot.

95. To kick off their heel run, what did the Road Warriors put in Dusty Rhodes' eye to injure it?
A. A finger
B. A spike
C. A hammer
D. A nail

96. Who did Dusty Rhodes team with to challenge the Road Warriors for their NWA World tag team title at Starrcade 1988?
A. Dustin Rhodes
B. The Ultimate Warrior
C. Sting
D. Randy Savage

97. What was the term used on WCW television for Vince Russo and Ed Ferrara when they first debuted?
   A. The Ultimate Power
   B. The Higher-Ups
   C. Management
   D. The Powers That Be

98. Who did Sting bring with him to Capitol Combat 1990 to combat the Four Horsemen?
   A. Sgt. Slaughter
   B. Cactus Jack
   C. Robocop
   D. Ric Flair

99. In the early nineties, The Wild Eyed Southern Boys tag team of Tracey Smothers and Steve Armstrong changed their name to what?
   A. The Hillbillies
   B. The Young Pistols
   C. The Bushwhackers
   D. The Young Guns

100. Rick Rude made his WCW return in 1991 under a mask. What was the masked man's name?
   A. The Halloween Phantom
   B. The Masked Avenger
   C. The Phantom
   D. Pumpkinhead

101. What was Van Hammer's nickname when he debuted for WCW?
   A. The Hammer
   B. The German Hammer
   C. Thor
   D. Heavy Metal

102. Big Van Vader defeated Sting at SuperBrawl III in what type of strap match?
   A. White Castle of Fear
   B. White Castle of Death
   C. The Leather Strap Match
   D. The Double Strap Match

103. In the early nineties, the WWF's Godwinn Brothers wrestled in WCW under what names?

A. Tex Cobb and Frenchie McFarlane
B. Leather Tex and The Marauder
C. Tex Slazenger and Shanghai Pierce
D. Joe Six-Pack and Couch Potato

104. What were the original names of Booker T and Stevie Ray when they debuted in WCW as Harlem Heat?
A. The Butcher and The Baker
B. Kane and Kole
C. LeeRoy Brown and Bad Ass Brown
D. King Mumba and Prince Kanda

105. In the first "Spin The Wheel, Make The Deal" match at Halloween Havoc 1992 between Jake Roberts and Sting, what match did the wheel select?
A. Strap Match
B. Coal Miner's Glove
C. Steel Cage
D. Barb Wire

106. In the second "Spin The Wheel, Make The Deal" match at Halloween Havoc 1993, what match did the wheel select?
A. Coal Miner's Glove
B. Chef's Knife Match
C. Texas Death Match
D. Dumpster Match

107. Who wrestled the second "Spin The Wheel, Make The Deal" match at Halloween Havoc 1993?
A. The Giant and Scott Hall
B. Diesel and Cactus Jack
C. Sting and Rick Rude
D. Big Van Vader and Cactus Jack

108. The Big Bossman made his WCW return in 1993, but changed his name to what?
A. The Boss
B. The Big Man
C. The Man
D. The Boss of Bosses

109. What was the name of Chavo Guerrero's wooden horse?
A. Tonto

B. Pinto

C. Chavez

D. Pepe

110. After Brutus Beefcake turned on Hulk Hogan at Halloween Havoc 1994, what name did he adopt?
A. The Butcher
B. The Baker
C. The Candlestick Maker
D. The Barber

111. What was Earthquake's initial gimmick when he made his 1994 WCW debut?
A. The Tremor
B. The Richter Scale
C. The Landslide
D. The Avalanche

112. Who was Goldberg's first pay-per-view challenger after he won the WCW World title?
A. Sting
B. Hulk Hogan
C. Curt Hennig
D. Randy Savage

113. How many Clash of the Champions did WCW air?
A. 22
B. 28
C. 35
D. 39

114. After the NWA pulled recognition of their title in WCW in 1993, what was the "gold belt" known as?
A. The Intercontinental World Title
B. International World Title
C. The Hardcore Title
D. The Cruiserweight Title

115. Who did Goldberg defeat to start his famed WCW unbeaten streak?
A. Lord Steven Regal
B. Hugh Morrus
C. Raven
D. Vincent

116. What was Kwee-Wee's alter ego?
    A. Alan Funk
    B. Mortimer Plumtree
    C. "Adorable" Alan
    D. Adam Windsor

117. Which WCW announcer was known as "The Professor"?
    A. Mike Tenay
    B. Tony Schiavone
    C. Scott Hudson
    D. Bobby Heenan

118. What was Mike Awesome's gimmick in WCW?
    A. The Fat Chick Thriller
    B. That Seventies Guy
    C. Career Killer
    D. All of the above

WWF

Every sport has its 800-pound gorilla in one form or another. Often it's a player's union or a commissioner or even a franchise owner. In the sports entertainment field of professional wrestling, it's the World Wrestling Federation.

The WWF is the single most important, influential organization in the history of professional wrestling. Sure, before the groundwork for the WWF was even an idea there was the NWA. But in the 1940s and 50s Vince McMahon, Sr. teamed with Toots Mondt to form Capitol Wrestling in Washington, D.C.

That's when McMahon, Sr. tapped into what would become the most important piece to the wrestling puzzle: cable television. The area in which Capitol Wrestling operated (the eastern seaboard) just so happened to be the area where the United States' first coaxial cable television system was being put in place. Capitol Wrestling's alliance with cable television was so successful that by 1963, McMahon and Mondt formed the World Wide Wrestling Federation (WWWF). Soon after, Mondt sold his share in the WWWF to McMahon.

Then the real power of the WWF was displayed. In 1983, McMahon, Sr. sold his interest in the federation (now called the WWF) to his son, Vince McMahon, Jr. From then on McMahon, Jr. was committed to spreading the WWF across the country, and he did so with cable television exposure, keen promotion and marketing which eliminated his competitors. In 1984 there were 20 regional wrestling promoters, by 1989 there were fewer than five.

The rest is history. Since the 1980s, the WWF has been synonymous with pro wrestling, thanks to the popularity of the WrestleMania events and timely marketing of the WWF's colorful stars. But the WWF's greatest promotional tool came in the form of a 6-foot-8-inch, 300-pound blond monster combining size, athleticism and charisma as never seen before. His name? Hulk Hogan. The rise of the WWF to the pinnacle of sports entertainment and the rise of Hulk Hogan as one of the most recognizable entertainers in the world were no coincidence. Both benefited from the success of the other.

The timing was perfect for the WWF. McMahon, Jr.'s slick marketing and promotion needed something more; something special to help the WWF dominate its competition, and Hulk Hogan fit that bill. Sure, the WCW made a punch in the 1990s thanks to the deep pockets of Ted Turner, but in

the end, the WWF prevailed yet again: the WCW was bought by Vince and the WWF in March of 2001.

But what's next for the WWF? Many believe wrestling has peaked, as PPV and television numbers seem to have plateaued. Don't look for the WWF to close up shop just yet. McMahon, Jr.'s ability to captivate his fans and create new and exciting storylines is sure to continue, and the addition of the WCW talent now thrown into the mix should provide the extra spark the WWF needs to remain at the top of the heap.

1. Who defeated Hulk Hogan in 1990 at WrestleMania 6 to win the WWF title?
   A. "Mr. Wonderful" Paul Orndorff
   B. Rowdy Roddy Piper
   C. "Macho Man" Randy Savage
   D. The Ultimate Warrior

2. Which two wrestlers combined to form the tag team duo called "The New Age Outlaws"?
   A. X-Pac and Billy Gunn
   B. Road Dogg and RVD
   C. Road Dogg and Billy Gunn
   D. X-Pac and Road Dogg

3. True or False: Kane won the "Inferno of Fire" match against The Undertaker at WrestleMania in 1998.

4. True or False: Razor Ramon won the Ladder Match in 1994 at WrestleMania against Shawn Michaels for the Intercontinental title.

5. Mr. T teamed with Hulk Hogan in WrestleMania 1 to defeat which tag team duo?
   A. The British Bulldogs
   B. "Mr. Wonderful" Paul Orndorff and Roddy Piper
   C. Demolition
   D. "Macho Man" Randy Savage and Lanny Poffo

6. True or False: Val Venis, who claimed to be an adult film star prior to becoming a wrestler, held the Hardcore Championship in 1998 and 1999.

7. According to a bizarre story line, which WWF wrestler impregnated a 79-year-old wrestler named Mae Young?
   A. Mark Henry
   B. Val Venis
   C. Triple H
   D. Grandmaster Sexay

8. In a bikini match against Jacqueline, what was special about Sable's bikini top?
   A. It was see-through
   B. It was too small
   C. It was on backwards
   D. It was painted on

9. Debra McMichael won the WWF women's title in 1999. What other three "titles" did Debra McMichael also once hold?
   A. Miss Illinois
   B. Miss Hawaiian Tropic
   C. Miss Texas USA
   D. Mrs. Mongo
   E. Miss Hooters
   F. Miss Nude USA
   G. Mrs. Vince McMahon

10. In the 1980s, Big John Studd offered $10,000 to anyone who could body slam him, an amount which was upped to $15,000 at WrestleMania. Who was the wrestler to slam the 6' 9", 365-pound Studd?
    A. Hulk Hogan
    B. Andre the Giant
    C. King Kong Bundy
    D. Hillbilly Jim

11. By what name is Davey Boy Smith better known?
    A. The Ultimate Warrior
    B. Buff Bagwell
    C. Mr. Wonderful
    D. The British Bulldog

12. Who became the first ever WWF European Champion in 1997?
    A. Rowdy Roddy Piper
    B. The Dynamite Kid
    C. The British Bulldog
    D. The Iron Sheik

13. With whom did Davey Boy Smith team to form the tag team duo called The British Bulldogs?
    A. Rowdy Roddy Piper
    B. The Dynamite Kid
    C. The Junkyard Dog
    D. Road Dogg

14. What tag team duo did The British Bulldogs defeat at WrestleMania 2 to win the tag team title?
    A. Greg Valentine and Brutus Beefcake
    B. Demolition
    C. The Hart Foundation
    D. Hulk Hogan and "Macho Man" Randy Savage

15. What were the names of the two wrestlers who made up the tag team called The Natural Disasters?
    A. Hurricane and Blizzard
    B. Tsunami and Landslide
    C. Typhoon and Earthquake
    D. Avalanche and Tidal Wave

16. The Rock teamed with what unlikely partner to win the WWF tag team belt three times in 1999?
    A. Mankind
    B. Stone Cold Steve Austin
    C. D-Lo Brown
    D. Mark Henry
    E. Triple H

17. Leapin' Lanny Poffo and The Genius are both characters assumed by what wrestling superstar's brother?
    A. Hulk Hogan
    B. "Macho Man" Randy Savage
    C. Kerry von Erich
    D. The Ultimate Warrior

18. Which wrestler won the WWF title in 2000 but his victory was not recognized by the WWF?
    A. Triple H
    B. Kurt Angle
    C. Stone Cold Steve Austin
    D. Chris Jericho

19. Which wrestler won the WWF Intercontinental title in 1990 AFTER his right foot was amputated?
    A. Cactus Jack
    B. The Ultimate Warrior
    C. Kerry von Erich
    D. Sgt. Slaughter

20. Where was the first WWF WrestleMania held?
    A. Nassau Coliseum
    B. Madison Square Garden
    C. Trump Plaza
    D. Silverdome
    E. Sports Arena
    F. The Horizon

21. Who was the Special Guest Ref in the main event?
    A. Hulk Hogan
    B. Vince McMahon
    C. Sgt. Slaughter
    D. Andre the Giant
    E. Bobby Heenan
    F. Muhammad Ali

22. Who won the 2nd Royal Rumble?
    A. Bret Hart
    B. Hulk Hogan
    C. Hacksaw Jim Duggan
    D. Big John Studd
    E. Ric Flair
    F. Lex Luger

23. When was the last WWF In Your House?
    A. 1995
    B. 1996
    C. 1997
    D. 1998

24. Where is the WWF headquarters?
    A. Stamford, Connecticut
    B. New York, New York
    C. Los Angeles, California
    D. Philadelphia, Pennsylvania

25. Who did Stone Cold Steve Austin defeat AFTER breaking his neck in the ring during that same match?
    A. Bret Hart
    B. Goldust
    C. Owen Hart
    D. The Undertaker

26. Who pinned Hulk Hogan at WrestleMania 6 in Toronto?
    A. Randy "Macho Man" Savage
    B. The Ultimate Warrior
    C. Big John Studd
    D. The Iron Sheik

27. What year did Chyna make her debut in the WWF?
    A. 1997
    B. 1998
    C. 1996
    D. 1995
    E. 1999

28. In what year did WrestleMania 1 take place?
    A. 1984
    B. 1985
    C. 1986
    D. 1987
    E. 1983

29. What Intercontinental champion did "The Junkyard Dog" defeat by countout in WrestleMania 1?
    A. Ricky "The Dragon" Steamboat
    B. Jimmy "Superfly" Snuka
    C. Greg "The Hammer" Valentine
    D. Tito Santana

30. What was the name of the tag team of Mankind and The Rock?
    A. Socko and Rocko
    B. Rock 'Em Sock 'Em
    C. Rock 'N Roll
    D. The People's Sock
    E. The Rock and Sock Connection

31. Which two wrestlers won the tag team title at WrestleMania 1?
    A. Randy "Macho Man" Savage and Hulk Hogan

B. Big John Studd and Hillbilly Jim
C. Jake "The Snake" Roberts and Brutus Beefcake
D. The Iron Sheik and Nikolai Volkoff

32. Why did George "The Animal" Steele only wrestle in the summer?
    A. He was a high school gym teacher
    B. He was a ski instructor in the winter
    C. He only liked warm weather
    D. He drove a snow plow in the winter

33. Who were the last three to remain in the 1998 Royal Rumble match?
    A. Mark Henry
    B. Rocky Maivia
    C. Steve Austin
    D. Farooq
    E. Dude Love

34. In the 1989 King of the Ring, who won the finals?
    A. Tito Santana
    B. Jimmy "Superfly" Snuka
    C. "The Model" Rick Martel
    D. Akeem

35. Who successfully defended the European Championship at
    Wrestlemania XIV?
    A. Marc Mero
    B. The Rock
    C. Triple H
    D. Owen Hart
    E. Ken Shamrock

36. Who won the 1989 Royal Rumble?
    A. The Warlord
    B. Hulk Hogan
    C. Rick Martel
    D. Ted DiBiase
    E. Hercules
    F. Big John Studd

37. At Wrestlemania XVI, who did NOT at one time hold the hardcore
    championship belt?
    A. Joey Abs
    B. Tazz

C. Crash Holly
D. Farooq
E. Hardcore Holly

38. What was the result of the 60-minute iron match at Judgement Day 2000?
A. Triple H won 6 falls to 5 over The Rock
B. The Rock won 7 falls to 4 over Triple H
C. Triple H won 8 falls to 7 over The Rock
D. The Rock won 6 falls to 4 over Triple H

39. Who were the last two men in the 20-man battle royal at Wrestlemania IV?
A. Junkyard Dog
B. Bret Hart
C. Nikolai Volkoff
D. Bad News Brown
E. Ron Bass
F. George "The Animal" Steele

40. Who won the tag team championship match at Wrestlemania VI?
A. Orient Express
B. Colossal Connection
C. Demolition
D. Hart Foundation
E. The Rockers

41. Which championship title match at Summerslam 1990 was decided in two out of three falls?
A. WWF heavyweight championship
B. WWF intercontinental championship
C. WWF tag team championship

42. In the 1993 King of the Ring, which two men battled to a time limit draw?
A. Bam Bam Bigelow
B. Mr. Perfect
C. "Hacksaw" Jim Duggan
D. Razor Ramon
E. Lex Luger
F. Bret "Hit Man" Hart
G. Tatanka
H. Mr. Hughes

43. Which match at Royal Rumble 1990 ended in a double disqualification?
    A. The Bushwhackers Vs. Rougeau Bros.
    B. Brutus Beefcake Vs. The Genius
    C. Ronnie Garvin Vs. Greg Valentine
    D. Jim Duggan Vs. Big Boss Man

44. At Survivor Series 1993, who survived All Americans Vs. Foreign Fanatics?
    A. Rick Steiner
    B. Yokozuna
    C. Crush
    D. Lex Luger
    E. Jacques from the Quebecers
    F. Ludvig Borga
    G. The Undertaker
    H. Scott Steiner

45. Who won the Intercontinental Championship match at Wrestlemania V?
    A. Jim Duggan
    B. Jake Roberts
    C. Ultimate Warrior
    D. Andre the Giant
    E. Rick Rude

46. Who successfully defended the Intercontinental Championship at Wrestlemania II?
    A. George "The Animal" Steele
    B. Don Muraco
    C. Paul Orndorff
    D. Randy Savage
    E. George Wells
    F. Jake Roberts

47. At Summerslam 1998, who won the Intercontinental Championship match?
    A. Rocky "The Rock" Maivia
    B. Marc Mero
    C. Mankind
    D. Triple H
    E. Ken Shamrock

48. Who were the last three remaining in the 1996 Royal Rumble match?
    A. Fatu
    B. Kama
    C. Isaac Yankeem
    D. Duke "The Dumpster" Droese
    E. Shawn Michaels
    F. The British Bulldog
    G. Diesel

49. Which team successfully defended the Tag Team Championship at Wrestlemania V?
    A. Hart Foundation
    B. Demolition
    C. Powers of Pain
    D. Rhythm and Blues

50. Who were the first two to enter the 1995 Royal Rumble?
    A. "British Bulldog" Davey Boy Smith
    B. Duke "The Dumpster" Droese
    C. "King of Harts" Owen Hart
    D. Timothy Well of Well Dunn
    E. Rick "The Model" Martel
    F. Shawn Michaels
    G. Jimmy DelRay of the Heavenly Bodies

51. At Wrestlemania VII, which two men battled in a career-ending match?
    A. Hulk Hogan
    B. "Macho King" Randy Savage
    C. The Ultimate Warrior
    D. Mr. Perfect
    E. Jake "The Snake" Roberts
    F. Rick "The Model" Martel
    G. Big Boss Man

52. Who won the Tag Team championship at Wrestlemania IV?
    A. Hart Foundation
    B. Demolition
    C. Islanders
    D. Strike Force
    E. The British Bulldogs

53. At the 1999 Royal Rumble, who won the WWF Intercontinental
   Championship match?
   A. Ken Shamrock
   B. "The Road Dog" Jesse James
   C. Gangrel
   D. The Big Boss Man
   E. "Bad Ass" Billy Gunn

54. At Royal Rumble 1991, who defeated The Ultimate Warrior for the
   WWF Heavyweight Championship?
   A. Bret "Hit Man" Hart
   B. The Mountie
   C. The Big Boss Man
   D. Hulk Hogan
   E. Sgt. Slaughter
   F. Randy "Macho King" Savage

55. Which were the two partners of Hillbilly Jim at Wrestlemania III?
   A. Little Tokyo
   B. The Haiti Kid
   C. Lord Littlebro
   D. Little Beaver

56. At In Your House XVI in 1997, who won the WWF Heavyweight
   Championship match?
   A. Shawn Michaels
   B. "Stone Cold" Steve Austin
   C. Vader
   D. Owen Hart
   E. Undertaker
   F. Sycho Sid

57. Who was victorious in the triple threat WWF Heavyweight
   Championship match at Summerslam 1999?
   A. Mankind
   B. Triple H
   C. Stone Cold Steve Austin

58. While WWF champion in the late 1970s and early 80s, Bob Backlund
   was referred to as what?
   A. The Minnesota Wonder
   B. The Upset Kid
   C. The All-American Boy

D. Man of 1,000 Holds

59. What former WCW star made his WWF debut on St. Valentine's Day Massacre on February 14, 1999?
    A. The Big Show/The Giant
    B. Chris Jericho
    C. Chris Benoit
    D. None of the above

60. Who briefly managed the Powers of Pain when they debuted in the WWF?
    A. Frenchie Martin
    B. Slick
    C. Bobby "The Brain" Heenan
    D. Baron Von Raschke

61. How did Brother Love greet the audience and his interview subjects?
    A. "I Love You"
    B. "All You Need Is Love"
    C. "Love Me"
    D. "I Love To Love"

62. What did Kamala eat on a broadcast of *Tuesday Night Titans*?
    A. Worms
    B. Sardines
    C. Raw Frog Legs
    D. Live Chicken

63. Who was Jake Roberts' first Wrestlemania opponent?
    A. Honky Tonk Man
    B. George Wells
    C. Barry Horowitz
    D. The Executioner

64. What was Jeff Jarrett's hit single during his WWF run as a country music singer wannabe?
    A. "With My Baby Tonight"
    B. "The Greatest Singer"
    C. "Nashville Is My Town"
    D. "The Double J Blues"

65. Who was The Undertaker's original manager?
    A. Paul Bearer

B. Ted DiBiase
C. Slick
D. Brother Love

66. Wrestlemania 2 took place in Rosemont, Illinois, Los Angeles, California, and what other city?
    A. Uniondale, New Jersey
    B. Boston, Massachusetts
    C. New York, NY
    D. Baltimore, Maryland

67. Which man was never "King" of the WWF?
    A. Haku
    B. "Hacksaw" Jim Duggan
    C. Harley Race
    D. All of the above were "Kings"

68. What was the special stipulation for the Wrestlemania 7 match between Jake Roberts and Rick Martel?
    A. Dog collar
    B. Ladder
    C. Blindfold
    D. No disqualification

69. In his theme song, The Mountie professed to be handsome, brave, and what?
    A. Strong
    B. Daring
    C. Mighty
    D. Dashing

70. The Can-Am Connection was composed of Rick Martel and what other wrestler?
    A. Tito Santana
    B. Jim Brunzell
    C. Bret Hart
    D. Tom Zenk

71. What was the name of Legion of Doom's ventriloquist's dummy in the WWF?
    A. Charlie
    B. Pauly
    C. Sluggo
    D. Rocco

72. Before coming to the WWF, what was Crash Holly's gimmick?
    A. Lucky Charms
    B. Erin O'Grady
    C. Chief O'Hara
    D. The Evil Leprechaun

73. Who won the Wrestlemania X Seven Gimmick Battle Royal?
    A. Sergeant Slaughter
    B. Nikolai Volkoff
    C. The Iron Sheik
    D. The Gobbledy Gooker

74. Which was not an interview segment on WWF television?
    A. The Flower Shop
    B. The Barber Shop
    C. The Snakepit
    D. The Truck Stop

75. Who was Sergeant Slaughter's manager during his WWF run as a heel in the early 1990s?
    A. General Adnan
    B. Slick
    C. Ted DiBiase
    D. The Iron Sheik

76. After Roddy Piper's retirement match victory at Wrestlemania 3, who helped Piper cut off the hair of "Adorable" Adrian Adonis?
    A. Hulk Hogan
    B. Jesse Ventura
    C. Brutus Beefcake
    D. The entire WWF roster

77. What famed boxer refereed the Hulk Hogan-Randy Savage bout that aired live on NBC on February 23, 1990?
    A. Mike Tyson
    B. Buster Douglas
    C. Muhammad Ali
    D. George Foreman

78. According to WWF storylines, what was Val Venis' former profession?
    A. Adult Film Star
    B. Plumber
    C. Country Music Star

D. Hockey Player

79. Who teamed with Nikolai Volkoff to form The Bolsheviks?
    A. Ivan Koloff
    B. Boris Zukov
    C. Krusher Kruschev
    D. Nikita Koloff

80. What "diet product" did Buddy Rose advertise in the WWF?
    A. Fat Away
    B. Eat Away
    C. Blow Away
    D. Diet Away

81. In the WWF, Kerry Von Erich was known as...
    A. The Texas Tornado
    B. The Modern-Day Warrior
    C. Courageous Kerry
    D. Texas Thunder

82. What show preceded *WWF Monday Night Raw*?
    A. *Wrestling Challenge*
    B. *Prime Time Wrestling*
    C. *Wrestling Superstars*
    D. *Superstars of Wrestling*

83. Who managed "Mr. Perfect" Curt Hennig in the WWF?
    A. Bobby Heenan
    B. "Coach" John Tolos
    C. The Genius
    D. All of the above

84. Instead of a three-count, what did King Kong Bundy insist upon?
    A. Five-count
    B. Ten-count
    C. One-count
    D. Two-count

85. Who feuded with Andre the Giant over who was the "Real Giant"?
    A. Hulk Hogan
    B. Big John Studd
    C. Blackjack Mulligan
    D. Bruiser Brody

86. What was Eddy Guerrero's pet name for Chyna?
    A. Wonder Woman
    B. Rose Petal
    C. Amazon Babe
    D. Mamacita

87. Who was the first King of the Ring?
    A. Bret Hart
    B. Owen Hart
    C. Jerry Lawler
    D. Steve Austin

88. The Ultimate Warrior destroyed the set of what interview segment?
    A. The Flower Shop
    B. Piper's Pit
    C. Brother Love
    D. The Barber Shop

89. What did announcer Jesse Ventura say about Hulkamania following Hulk Hogan's world title loss to the Ultimate Warrior at Wrestlemania 6?
    A. "Hulkamania is dead!"
    B. "Good riddance, Hulkamania!"
    C. "Hulkamania sucks!"
    D. "I guess Hulkamania will live forever!"

90. True or False: Terry Funk has also wrestled as "Chainsaw Charlie."

91. True or False: Barry "Smash" Darsow was a founding member of Demolition.

92. True or False: The 1988 Royal Rumble was one of the WWF's first pay-per-views.

93. True or False: Michael Hayes briefly managed The Hardy Boyz.

94. True or False: Zeus wrestled in the main event of Summerslam 1988.

95. What was the name of the stuffed animal that George "The Animal" Steele carried to the ring?
    A. Friend
    B. Mine
    C. Dog
    D. Animal

96. Which wrestling manager briefly had his own WWF program?
    A. Jimmy Hart
    B. Paul Bearer
    C. Bobby "The Brain" Heenan
    D. Freddie Vlassie

97. Who replaced Brutus Beefcake in Johnny Valiant's "Dream Team?
    A. Dino Bravo
    B. Jake "The Snake" Roberts
    C. Razor Ramon
    D. Ricky "The Dragon" Steamboat

98. Who did The Honky Tonk Man defeat for the WWF Intercontinental title?
    A. The Junkyard Dog
    B. Tito Santana
    C. Jimmy "Superfly" Snuka
    D. Ricky "The Dragon" Steamboat

99. Who was Dusty Rhodes' valet during his 1989 - 1991 WWF run?
    A. Miss Elizabeth
    B. Sapphire
    C. Debra McMichael
    D. Tammy Sytch

100. Honky Tonk Man and Greg "The Hammer" Valentine formed what tag team?
    A. The Honkys
    B. Love and War
    C. The Honky Hearts
    D. Rhythm and Blues

101. Who was Triple H's butler early in his WWF run?
    A. Geevs
    B. Mr. Hughes
    C. Mr. Helmsley
    D. Sycho Sid

MISCELLANEOUS

Q: What is the most predictable thing about professional wrestling today?

A: It is totally unpredictable. That simple truth is what inspired us to create this chapter of trivia. It's a mish-mash, a hodge-podge, a grouping of things that refuse to be defined.

We've broken this book down into some basic categories that are rather obvious to wrestling fans: the WWF, the WCW, International, Old School, and The Name Game. But true wrestling fans know that the best parts of professional wrestling cannot be packaged into nice, neat little chapters. Much of what we all love about wrestling is its insanity. It creates a fantasy world within which the inhabitants do the unthinkable...and get away with it!

When creating and compiling all of these trivia questions, we found that there is so much great wrestling stuff out there that doesn't fit our formula. But we needed to include it somehow. Thus, we have this chapter in the back of the book called, what else, Miscellaneous. Where else would you put questions like 'What piece of dinnerware does Abdullah the Butcher most often use to scratch and cut his head?' and 'Before he became a wrestler, Hulk Hogan was in a rock band. What instrument did he play?'

These tidbits of information and unusual trivia are often the best parts of wrestling. They're unexpected and unpredictable and add spontaneity to everything.

Q: Which 1960s wrestler, believed by many to be the heaviest ever, supposedly once wrestled at a weight of over 800 pounds? A: Happy Humphrey

Q: Who was the first ECW champion? A: Jimmy "Superfly" Snuka.

That is just a taste of the trivia oddities and strangely compelling information you'll find within this chapter.

As an added bonus, at the end of this section are lists detailing the heights and weights of your favorite wrestlers, an explanation of the wrestling relatives found within the various federations (including whether or not the relation is real or just a part of a story line), and a great compilation of the names of the finishing moves and/or signature moves of almost every wrestler around.

71

1. What did The Godfather offer to his opponent before each match to ensure a forfeit win?
   A. Money
   B. A job
   C. Two of his "ho's"
   D. An offer he couldn't refuse

2. Muhammad Ali once said that his outrageous persona was influenced by which wrestler?
   A. Goldust
   B. Gorilla Monsoon
   C. Rowdy Roddy Piper
   D. Gorgeous George

3. How were The Bushwhackers related?
   A. Cousins
   B. Father and son
   C. Brothers
   D. Uncle and nephew

4. What type of bird did Koko B. Ware bring into the ring and dance with before each match?
   A. An eagle
   B. A cockatoo
   C. A parrot
   D. A peacock

5. Cactus Jack has competed in some of the most dangerous wrestling matches ever. What was special about the ring in which Cactus Jack won the 1995 King of the Death Match tournament?
   A. It was covered in barbed wire
   B. It was on fire
   C. It was a mine field
   D. It was inside a cage

6. What piece of dinnerware does Abdullah the Butcher most often use to scratch and cut his head?
   A. Knife
   B. Spoon
   C. Ladle
   D. Fork

7. Before he became a wrestler, Hulk Hogan was in a rock band. What instrument did he play?
   A. Drums
   B. Bass guitar
   C. Guitar
   D. Keyboard

8. Legendary manager Jimmy Hart wears ties emblazoned with piano keys. What was the name of the music group he was a part of in the 1960s?
   A. Quiet Riot
   B. The Hart Foundation
   C. The Gentrys
   D. Heart

9. What was the name of the song by Jimmy Hart's band which broke into the Top 10 in 1965?
   A. "Ain't Nothin' But a G Thang"
   B. "Keep on Rockin' "
   C. "Rock Around the Clock"
   D. "Keep on Dancing"

10. Who is the only NFL player to have held a wrestling world title and was elected to the Pro Football Hall of Fame?
    A. Bronko Nagurski
    B. Lawrence Taylor
    C. Steve "Mongo" McMichael
    D. William "The Refrigerator" Perry

11. True or False: Kevin Nash, known as "Big Sexy" to his female fans, has appeared in adult films including *Headlock*, a hardcore wrestling movie.

12. Which wrestler in the 1990s earned the nickname "Puke"?
    A. Diamond Dallas Page
    B. Darren Drozdov
    C. Perry Saturn
    D. X-Pac

13. Adore & Envie and Hollywood & Vine were tag team duos in what now defunct wrestling organization?
    A. N.W.W.A. (National Women's Wrestling Asssociation)
    B. E.C.W.W. (Extreme Championship Women's Wrestling)

C. G.L.O.W. (Gorgeous Ladies of Wrestling)
D. W.O.W. (Women of Wrestling)

14. Many wrestlers have claimed to be Native Americans over the years. But to which Indian tribe did Tiger Nelson, an African-American, claim to
be a member?
   A. The Blackfoot Tribe
   B. The Afro Tribe
   C. The Jive Tribe
   D. The Apache Tribe

15. D-Lo Brown's finishing move, a splash, carries what name?
   A. The Splatter
   B. D-Splash
   C. The Lo-Down
   D. The Lo-Down-Dirty Splash

16. Which broadcaster dubbed Debra McMichael's breasts "puppies"?
   A. Bobby "The Brain" Heenan
   B. Jerry "The King" Lawler
   C. Mean Gene Oakerlund
   D. Shane McMahon

17. What is the name of Little Spike Dudley's finishing move?
   A. The Railroad Spike
   B. The Dudley Dunk
   C. The Little Spikey
   D. The Dudley Dog

18. What big nickname has the diminutive wrestler Reckless Youth earned with his myriad of moves?
   A. The Big Wreck
   B. The King of the Independents
   C. The Wrecking Ball
   D. The Multiple Moves Maniac

19. Which 1960s wrestler, believed by many to be the heaviest ever, supposedly once wrestled at a weight of over 800 pounds?
   A. Yokozuna
   B. Andre the Giant
   C. Happy Humphrey
   D. King Kong Bundy

20. What tag team reportedly tipped the scales at or over 727 pounds...each?
    A. The McGuyire Twins
    B. The Natural Disasters
    C. Demolition
    D. Andre the Giant and Big John Studd

21. Known for his enormous size, King Kong Bundy reportedly did what during a match in New York against Primo Carnera III?
    A. Pooped his pants
    B. Broke his butt
    C. Broke the ring
    D. Threw up

22. Who was the tallest man in pro wrestling history?
    A. Andre the Giant
    B. El Gigante Gonzalez
    C. Paul Wight
    D. Kevin Nash

23. Wrestlers have always been known to enjoy a drink now and then. Even Stone Cold Steve Austin often brings beers into the ring with him. But, which wrestler reportedly once drank 117 beers at one sitting?
    A. Yokozuna
    B. Bruno Sammartino
    C. El Gigante Gonzalez
    D. Andre the Giant

24. At which Division I school did Kevin Nash play basketball?
    A. University of Tennessee
    B. University of Kentucky
    C. North Carolina University
    D. University of Virginia

25. Which two super-tall wrestlers once teamed up to form the tag team called The Skyscrapers?
    A. Sid Vicious and Kevin Nash
    B. Sid Vicious and Dan Spivey
    C. Kevin Nash and Scott Hall
    D. Big John Studd and Andre the Giant

26. Who was the first ever Heavyweight Champion in the ECW?
    A. Tito Santana
    B. Johnny Hot Body
    C. Sandman
    D. Jimmy "Superfly" Snuka

27. Despite all the wrestling federations and independent leagues, there are still just two elite wrestling organizations: the WWF and the WCW. All of the wrestlers listed below have won wrestling titles in various leagues, but ONLY ONE has held a world title in either the WWF or WCW. Who is it?
    A. Rowdy Roddy Piper
    B. Jimmy "Superfly" Snuka
    C. Gorgeous George
    D. The Sheik
    E. Fred Blassie
    F. Killer Kowalski
    G. Bobo Brazil
    H. King Kong Bundy
    I. Greg Valentine
    J. Stan Hensen
    K. Yokozuna

28. What is the name of Chris Jericho's finishing move?
    A. The Walls of Jericho
    B. Boston Clam Chowder
    C. The Jericho Jump
    D. The Leap of Faith

29. What is the name of Scott Steiner's finishing move?
    A. The Poppa Pump Punch
    B. The Steiner Whiner
    C. The Steiner Recliner
    D. The Steiner Stomp

30. What was the name of Ravishing Rick Rude's finishing move?
    A. The Rick Rash
    B. The Rude Awakening
    C. The Rude Ruckus
    D. The Lude Rude

31. Who did Bronko Nagurski beat to win his wrestling title?
    A. Lou Thesz

B. Verne Gagne
C. Gorgeous George
D. The Sheik

32. What is the name of Diamond Dallas Page's finishing move?
    A. The Page Turner
    B. The Diamond in the Ruff
    C. The Girl's Best Friend
    D. The Diamond Cutter

33. What is the name of Perry Saturn's finishing move?
    A. Space Mountain
    B. The Perry Pulverizer
    C. The Rings of Saturn
    D. The Saturn Suplex

34. What is the name of Lex Luger's finishing move?
    A. The Lex Leap
    B. The Luger Lunge
    C. The Torture Rack
    D. The Texas Torture

35. Who was the NWA champ during the first Clash of the Champions?
    A. Sting
    B. Lex Luger
    C. Steve Austin
    D. Brad Armstrong
    E. Hulk Hogan
    F. Ric Flair

36. About how many people watch wrestling on television every week?
    A. 10 million
    B. 100 million
    C. 63 million
    D. 36 million

37. What did the letters ECW originally stand for?
    A. Extreme Challenge Wrestling
    B. Eastern Championship Wrestling
    C. Eternal Challenge Wrestling
    D. Everywhere Championship Wrestling

38. True or False: When a wrestler uses a razor blade to cut his forehead, allowing the blood to flow over the face, it is called the "crimson mask" effect.

39. What is the term used to describe when a referee is knocked out of commission, allowing the wrestlers to do anything?
    A. A ref bump
    B. A ref check
    C. Cleaning the ring
    D. An RKO

40. Who does Mick Foley credit as the wrestler he most looked up to?
    A. Cactus Jack
    B. George "The Animal" Steele
    C. Jimmy "Superfly" Snuka
    D. Gorgeous George

41. What other federation did Vince McMahon create in the early 1990s?
    A. The World Bodybuilding Federation
    B. The Women's World Wrestling Federation
    C. The Arm Wrestling Federation
    D. The Thumb Wrestling Federation

42. Which wrestler had a metal plate inserted into his forearm after a motorcycle accident, and today uses it as a weapon in the ring?
    A. Randy Savage
    B. Ric Flair
    C. Hulk Hogan
    D. Lex Luger

43. For which university did Scott Hall play basketball?
    A. St. Joseph's University
    B. St. Mary's University
    C. University of Notre Dame
    D. Boston College

44. Which wrestler spent time as a minor league baseball player in the St. Louis Cardinals, Cincinnati Reds and Chicago White Sox organizations?
    A. Hacksaw Jim Duggan
    B. Leapin' Lanny Poffo
    C. "Macho Man" Randy Savage
    D. X-Pac

45. Who was the first African-American wrestler to win a world championship?
   A. Booker T
   B. Junkyard Dog
   C. The Rock
   D. Ron Simmons

46. Which wrestler was once known as Crusher Yircov?
   A. Nikolai Volkoff
   B. Bam Bam Bigelow
   C. Diamond Dallas Page
   D. Rikishi

47. Which wrestler is known for his tattooed head?
   A. Earthquake
   B. Balls Mahoney
   C. Bam Bam Bigelow
   D. Buh Buh Ray Dudley

48. What brand of beer does Stone Cold Steve Austin usually drink in the ring?
   A. Bud Light
   B. Miller Genuine Draft
   C. Coors
   D. Budweiser

49. What is the name of Triple H's finishing move?
   A. The Triple Hammer
   B. The Helmsley Hurricane
   C. The Pedigree
   D. The Blueblood

50. Chris Jericho's father is a former professional athlete. What sport did he play?
   A. Hockey
   B. Football
   C. Rugby
   D. Baseball

51. Whose nasty signature move is called "The Stink Face"?
   A. Gangrel
   B. Rikishi
   C. Raven
   D. Konnan

52. Which of the following character names has ECW star Raven NOT used in the past?
    A. Scotty the Body
    B. Johnny Polo
    C. The Crow
    D. All of the above

53. In 1999 Stone Cold Steve Austin defeated The Rock in a wild match. How many referees were knocked out?
    A. Three
    B. Two
    C. Five
    D. None

54. Who turned on Sting in 1990, ending his short tenure in the Four Horsemen?
    A. Ric Flair
    B. Arn Anderson
    C. Ole Anderson
    D. All of the above

55. Headbanger Mosh grew his hair out to portray what character based on a television show?
    A. Barney Fife
    B. Beaver Cleaver
    C. Agent Mulder
    D. Bart Simpson

56. True or False: Honky Tonk Man debuted in the WWF as a babyface.

57. True or False: Steve Austin turned on Brian Pillman after joining forces with Paul E. Dangerously.

58. True or False: Mike Enos and Wayne Bloom joined the WWF as Beau and Blake, the Beverly Brothers.

59. Which wrestler did not hold both the WWF and WCW World heavy-weight titles?
    A. Ric Flair
    B. The Giant/The Big Show
    C. Steve Austin
    D. Kevin Nash/Diesel

60. Who wrestled the first "Hell In The Cell" match?
    A. Shawn Michaels and Mick Foley
    B. Shawn Michaels and The Undertaker
    C. The Undertaker and Mick Foley
    D. Mick Foley and Terry Funk

61. How does a wrestler win a cage match?
    A. Exit through the cage door
    B. Go over the top of the cage to the floor below
    C. Pin his opponent
    D. All of the above

62. What was Steve Austin's original finishing move in the WWF?
    A. The Million Dollar Dream
    B. Stone Cold Stunner
    C. The Hot Shot
    D. The Figure Four

63. In what city did the first match between Hulk Hogan and Ric Flair take place?
    A. New York, NY
    B. Pittsburgh, PA
    C. St. Louis, MO
    D. Dayton, OH

64. How did Larry Zbyszko win his first AWA World heavyweight title?
    A. Tournament final
    B. Commissioner Decree
    C. Battle Royal
    D. Purchase

65. In 1996, Paul Bearer turned on The Undertaker to manage what wrestler?
    A. Mankind
    B. Kane
    C. Big Van Vader
    D. Yokozuna

66. How many wrestlers competed in the 1988 Royal Rumble?
    A. 30
    B. 20
    C. 25
    D. 40

67. How many consecutive weeks did Nitro defeat Raw in the ratings?
    A. 94
    B. 101
    C. 83
    D. 72

68. Who ended Triple H's first reign as WWF champion?
    A. Vince McMahon
    B. Mankind
    C. The Rock
    D. The Undertaker

69. Who defeated The Great Muta in 1993 to win the NWA heavyweight title?
    A. Ric Flair
    B. Barry Windham
    C. Rick Rude
    D. Jushin "Thunder" Liger

70. Who was the third member of Demolition?
    A. Crunch
    B. Crash
    C. Munch
    D. Crush

71. Which wrestler did Buff Bagwell team with to win the WCW World tag team title?
    A. The Patriot
    B. Shane Douglas
    C. 2 Cold Scorpio
    D. All of the above

72. True or False: Dusty Rhodes once wrestled under a mask as The Yellow Dog.

73. True or False: Mick Foley's WWF debut was as a jobber long before he became Mankind.

74. True or False: Nick Bockwinkel pinned Stan Hansen for the AWA World heavyweight title.

75. True or False: Ric Flair and Terry Funk ended their 1989 feud with an "I Quit" match.

76. True or False: Randy Savage's Wrestlemania debut was in a match against Ricky Steamboat.

77. True or False: Ric Flair defeated Barry Horowitz in his September 1991 WWF debut.

78. True or False: Ric Flair defeated Hulk Hogan in their first encounter in October of 1991.

79. True or False: In 1995, Monday Nitro debuted at CNN Center in Atlanta, Georgia.

80. True or False: In the first head-to-head encounter between Nitro and Raw, WCW defeated the WWF.

81. True or False: Rick Rude is the only wrestler to appear on Nitro and Raw on the same night.

82. True or False: Jesse Ventura refereed the 1999 Summerslam match where Triple H won the WWF World title.

83. True or False: Harvey Whippleman is a former WWF Women's champion.

84. True or False: Kurt Angle made his pay-per-view debut at the 1999 Royal Rumble.

85. True or False: Gorilla Monsoon and "Cowboy" Bill Watts are former WWWF World tag team champions.

86. Who ended Larry Zbyszko's first reign as AWA champion and lost the belt back to him?
    A. Rick Rude
    B. Road Dogg
    C. Dick the Bruiser
    D. Mr. Saito

87. After retiring the European title in 1999, Shane McMahon awarded the belt to what wrestler?

A. The British Bulldog
B. Mideon
C. Psicosis
D. Lord Steven Regal

88. Who was the final WCW World Television champion?
    A. Chris Benoit
    B. Shane Douglas
    C. Sid Vicious
    D. "Hacksaw" Jim Duggan

89. Who did Steve Austin and Brian Pillman defeat for their only WCW World Tag Team title?
    A. Sting and Diamond Dallas Page
    B. Ric Flair and Lex Luger
    C. Ricky Steamboat and Shane Douglas
    D. Big Show and Ric Flair

90. Who was the first ECW champion?
    A. Johnny Hot Body
    B. Jimmy "Superfly" Snuka
    C. Don Muraco
    D. Sabu

91. True or False: Ricky Morton and Bobby Fulton formed a tag team called The Fantastic Express.

92. What group did Eric Bischoff and Vince Russo form when they returned to WCW television in April 2000?
    A. The NWA
    B. The Management
    C. The New Blood
    D. The Next Generation

93. Who won the inaugural Royal Rumble?
    A. Goldberg
    B. Rey Misterio, Jr.
    C. Crash Holly
    D. "Hacksaw" Jim Duggan

94. At NWA Bloodfest (part 2) in 1993, how did the Don Muraco/Jimmy Snuka Vs. Public Enemy match end?

A. Pinfall
B. Disqualification
C. Count-out
D. Forfeit (by Public Enemy)

95. Which three men participated in the three-way dance singles match at Hardcore Heaven 2000?
A. Jerry Lynn
B. Masato Tanaka
C. Simon Diamond
D. Rob Can Dam
E. Little Guido
F. Mikey Whipwreck

96. Who defeated Tommy Rich at the 1997 event Crossing The Line Again?
A. Shane Douglas
B. Brian Lee
C. Rob van Dam
D. Terry Funk

97. Which two teams clashed in the Barbed-wire match at Heat Wave 1994?
A. Axl & Ian Rotten
B. Terry & Dory Funk, Jr
C. Public Enemy
D. Sabu & The Tazmanac
E. The Bruise Brothers
F. The Pitbulls

98. At When Worlds Collide in 1994, who was/were the winner(s) of the handicap elimination match?
A. Mr. Hughes
B. Shane Douglas
C. Public Enemy Rock
D. Public Enemy Grunge
E. J.T. Smith

99. Who won the ECW Championship Match at 1995 Double Tables?
A. Ian Rotten
B. Mikey Whipwreck
C. Tully Blanchard
D. Shane Douglas

E. Sandman

100. Who won the TV championship match at High Incident 1996?
    A. Tazz
    B. Shane Douglas
    C. Spike Dudley
    D. Sandman

101. Who won the ECW championship match at Heat Wave 1999?
    A. Jazz
    B. Super Crazy
    C. Tazz
    D. Yoshihiro Tajiri
    E. Nova

102. What kind of match was the ECW world championship match at A Matter of Respect 1996?
    A. Three-way dance
    B. Two out of three falls
    C. Steel-cage match
    D. Falls count anywhere

103. At Wrestlepalooza 1997, who participated in both TV championship matches?
    A. Shane Douglas
    B. Tazz
    C. Chris Candido
    D. Chris Chetti

104. At 1996's edition of November to Remember, who won the ECW tag team championship match?
    A. Public Enemy
    B. The Eliminators
    C. Sabu & Rob Van Dam
    D. The Gangstas

105. Who did Rob Van Dam wrestle in his ECW debut at House Party 1996?
    A. Axl Rotten
    B. Sabu
    C. Tazz
    D. Rey Misterio, Jr.

106. Which title match went to a time-limit draw at Cyberslam 1996?
    A. World championship
    B. TV championship
    C. Tag Team championship
    D. Heavyweight Championship

107. At Orgy of Violence 1997, who won the TV championship match?
    A. Kronus
    B. Rob Van Dam
    C. Shane Douglas
    D. Chris Candido
    E. Tazz

108. At Cyberslam 1998, who defeated Brakkus?
    A. Al Snow
    B. Tazz
    C. Justin Credible
    D. Doug Furnas

109. Which team won the tag team championship match at the 1996 event the Doctor Is In?
    A. The Eliminators
    B. The Gangstas
    C. The Bruise Brothers
    D. Samoan Gangsta Party

110. At 1999's Re-enter the Sandman, which championship belt was the first one up for grabs?
    A. Tag team championship
    B. TV championship
    C. Heavyweight championship

111. At Cyberslam 1999, how did the ECW championship match end?
    A. Submission
    B. Disqualification
    C. No contest
    D. Count-out
    E. Pinfall

112. Who walked away from Ultimate Jeopardy 1996 as the ECW champion?
    A. Sandman
    B. Tommy Dreamer
    C. Stevie Richards
    D. Brian Lee

113. Who won the TV championship match at Barely Legal 1997?
    A. Shane Douglas
    B. Tazz
    C. Pitbull #2
    D. Pitbull #1

114. At the "Last Show at the Madhouse" event in 1999, which championship match went to a no contest?
    A. Tag team championship
    B. Heavyweight championship
    C. TV championship

115. At 1996 Holiday Hell, who won the ECW championship match?
    A. Rob Van Dam
    B. Sabu
    C. Raven
    D. The Sandman

116. At the 1993 Summer Sizzler, who won the TV championship match?
    A. Tommy Cairo
    B. The Sandman
    C. Jimmy Snuka
    D. Don Murraco

117. At 1998 Hostile City Showdown, who won the four-way dance match?
    A. Buh Buh Ray & D-Von Dudley
    B. Rob Van Dam & Sabu
    C. Sandman & Tommy Dreamer
    D. Kronus & New Jack

118. At the 1997 event Better Than Ever, who was defeated by Al Snow?
    A. Paul Diamond
    B. Tazz
    C. Spike Dudley
    D. Justin Credible

119. Who left Barely Legal, ECW's first pay-per-view, as ECW World champion?
   A. Terry Funk
   B. Raven
   C. Sabu
   D. Shane Douglas

120. What was the relationship between Tommy Dreamer and Raven?
   A. Cousins
   B. Childhood friends
   C. Brothers
   D. Brothers-in-law

121. In ECW, Perry Saturn was part of what tag team?
   A. The Eliminators
   B. Public Enemy
   C. The Gangstas
   D. The Rings of Saturn

122. What style of wrestling does Steve Corino espouse?
   A. Hardcore
   B. Catch-As-Catch-Can
   C. Greco Roman
   D. Old School

123. What former WWF star interfered in the Hardcore Heaven 1997 match between Tommy Dreamer and Jerry Lawler?
   A. Sunny
   B. Rick Rude
   C. Jake Roberts
   D. All of the above

124. Who was not a Dudley Boy?
   A. Sign Guy Dudley
   B. Quintessential Dudley
   C. Dances With Dudley
   D. Big Dick Dudley

125. Who was the manager of the Dudley Boyz?
   A. Bill Alphonso
   B. Francine
   C. Big Daddy Dudley
   D. Joel Gertner

126. What was Jerry Lynn's nickname in ECW?
  A. The Real Deal
  B. The Whole F'in Show
  C. Gentleman
  D. The New F'in Show

127. Which wrestler was not a member of the Full Blooded Italians?
  A. Tommy Rich
  B. Spike Dudley
  C. Tracey Smothers
  D. Little Guido

128. When The Original Midnight Express "invaded" the NWA in 1988, who were its members?
  A. Dennis Condrey and Randy Rose
  B. Dennis Condrey and Bobby Eaton
  C. Dennis Condrey and Jack Victory
  D. Randy Rose and Norvell Austin

129. According to his character, who did Jim Cornette rely on for monetary support?
  A. Grandmother
  B. Mother
  C. Aunt
  D. Great Grandmother

130. What was the name of Hulk Hogan's short-lived restaurant that opened at the Mall of America in 1995?
  A. HulkBurgers
  B. Hulk Hogan's Pastamania
  C. HulkDogs
  D. The Hulkster's Family Restaurant

131. What group of upstart rookies from the Power Plant was formed by Mike Sanders, Chuck Palumbo, Shawn Stasiak, and others?
  A. New Blood
  B. The Upstarts
  C. Natural Born Thrillers
  D. Power Plant Alumni

132. What NWA program competed with the 1988 Royal Rumble?
    A. Clash of the Champions
    B. Starrcade
    C. Bunkhouse Stampede
    D. Superstars On The SuperStation

133. True or False: Hulk Hogan is a former AWA World heavyweight champion.

134. True or False: Wrestler Kenny Jay was known as "Scrapiron."

135. True or False: Out of respect for The Bruiser, Bruiser Brody was known as "Boom Boom" Brody.

136. True or False: Jerry Lynn finally ended Rob Van Dam's nearly two-year reign as ECW World Television champion.

137. True or False: The Super Destroyers were the first ECW tag team champions.

138. True or False: Manager Bill Alphonso turned on Sabu at Barely Legal in April 1997.

LISTS OF WRESTLING TIDBITS

Wrestlers' Heights and Weights:

Below are the heights and weights of some of the best-known wrestlers of the last 15 years. Since these figures are subjective and depend somewhat on the accuracy of what is reported by the various federations, the heights and weights represent our best estimations. In addition, wrestlers' weights can fluctuate from match to match, so our figures represent a rough average of a wrestler's weight, and are again, an estimation.

Adam Bomb	6'6"	292 lbs.	Doug Furnas	5'11"	243 lbs.
Ahmed Johnson	6'2"	265 lbs.	Duke Droese	6'5"	306 lbs.
Aldo Montoya	6'0"	225 lbs.	Dusty Rhodes	6'3"	289 lbs.
Alex Porteau	5'10"	235 lbs.	Earthquake	6'4"	462 lbs.
Animal (LOD)	6'1"	285 lbs.	Eddy Guerrero	5'8"	221 lbs.
Andre the Giant	7'5"	520 lbs.	The Executioner	6'4"	289 lbs.
Arn Anderson	6'0"	249 lbs.	Faarooq	6'3"	272 lbs.
Bam Bam Bigelow	6'3"	368 lbs.	Flash Funk	5'11"	235 lbs.
Barry Horowitz	5'10"	227 lbs.	Freddie Joe Floyd	6'1"	227 lbs.
Bart Gunn	6'5"	260 lbs.	Giant Gonzales	7'7"	435 lbs.
Bill Goldberg	6'4"	290 lbs.	Greg "The Hammer" Valentine		
Billy Gunn	6'5"	254 lbs.		6'0"	248 lbs.
BlackJack Bradshaw	6'9"	309 lbs.	Hacksaw Jim Duggan	6'3"	280 lbs.
BlackJack Wyndham	6'5"	273 lbs.	Haku	6'0"	273 lbs.
Bob Backlund	6'1"	234 lbs.	Headbanger Mosh	6'0"	243 lbs.
Bob "Spark Plug" Holly	6'1"	231 lbs.	Headbanger Thrasher	6'2"	242 lbs.
			Henry O. Godwinn	6'7"	288 lbs.
Bret Hart	6'0"	234 lbs.	Hillbilly Jim	6'7"	286 lbs.
Brian Christopher	5'10"	230 lbs.	Honky Tonk Man	6'1"	258 lbs.
Brian Nobbs	6'1"	295 lbs.	Hulk Hogan	6'8"	303 lbs.
Brian Pillman	6'0"	226 lbs.	Triple H	6'4"	246 lbs.
British Bulldog	5'10"	253 lbs.	Iron Sheik	6'0"	262 lbs.
Brooklyn Brawler	6'0"	231 lbs.	Irwin R. Sheister	6'3"	248 lbs.
Brutus Beefcake	6'4"	271 lbs.	Jake "The Snake" Roberts		
Buff Bagwell	6'1"	240 lbs.		6'5"	253 lbs.
Bushwhacker Butch	6'0"	255 lbs.	Jeff Jarrett	5'10"	230 lbs.
Bushwhacker Luke	6'1"	244 lbs.	Jerry Saggs	6'3"	290 lbs.
Chris Benoit	5'10"	218 lbs.	Jerry Lawler	6'0"	234 lbs.
Bret Hart	5'10"	225 lbs.	Jesse James	6'4"	240 lbs.
Crush	6'6"	318 lbs.	Jim Duggan	6'3"	280 lbs.
Curt Hennig	6'3"	257 lbs.	Jimmy "Superfly" Snuka	6'0"	250 lbs.
Dean Douglas	6'0"	223 lbs.	Jim Neidhart	6'1"	281 lbs.
Dean Malenko	5'9"	216 lbs.	Kamala	6'7"	345 lbs.
DDP	6'5"	260 lbs.	Kama Mustafaa	6'6"	340 lbs.
Disco Inferno	6'0"	238 lbs.	Kane	6'7"	345 lbs.

Ken Shamrock	6'0	235 lbs.	Rick Steiner	5'11"	248 lbs.		
Kevin Nash	6'11"	356 lbs.	Rockabilly	6'3"	256 lbs.		
King Kong Bundy	6'4"	446 lbs.	Rocky Maivia	6'5"	275 lbs.		
Koko B. Ware	5'9"	229 lbs.	Salvatore Sincere	6'3"	250 lbs.		
Konnan	5'10"	237 lbs.	Savio Vega	5'10"	256 lbs.		
Leif Cassidy	6'1"	231 lbs.	Scott Hall	6'8"	290 lbs.		
Lex Luger	6'5"	265 lbs.	Scott Norton	6'3"	340 lbs.		
Mabel	6'10"	568 lbs.	Scott Steiner	6'1"	235 lbs.		
Mankind	6'3"	287 lbs.	Sgt. Slaughter	6'3"	310 lbs.		
Marc Mero	6'1"	235 lbs.	Shawn Michaels	6'0"	235 lbs.		
Marty Jannetty	5'11"	230 lbs.	Skip	5'8"	226 lbs.		
Meng	6'0"	273 lbs.	Stone Cold Steve Austin				
Mo	6'1"	285 lbs.		6'3"	256 lbs.		
Mr. Hughes	6'5"	308 lbs.	The Sultan	6'2"	260 lbs.		
Nailz	6'5"	271 lbs.	Sycho Sid	6'10"	313 lbs.		
Owen Hart	5'11"	227 lbs.	Tatanka	6'1"	250 lbs.		
Paul Roma	5'11"	235 lbs.	Terry Funk	6'1"	247 lbs.		
Philip LaFon	5'11"	235 lbs.	Tito Santana	6'1"	244 lbs.		
Phinneas I. Godwinn	6'7"	310 lbs.	T.L. Hopper	6'1"	235 lbs.		
Randy Savage	6'2"	245 lbs.	Ultimate Warrior	6'2"	275 lbs.		
Raven	6'1"	235 lbs.	The Undertaker	6'10"	328 lbs.		
Razor Ramon (Fake)	6'5"	285 lbs.	Vader	6'6"	452 lbs.		
Rey Misterio Jr	5'3"	140 lbs.	Vince	6'2"	250 lbs.		
Ric Flair	6'1"	243 lbs.	X-Pac	6'2"	212 lbs.		
Rick Martel	6'0"	234 lbs.	Yokozuna	6'4"	621 lbs.		
Rick Rude	6'3"	251 lbs.	Zip-The Bodydonnas	5'10"	220 lbs.		

Wrestling Relatives
(Brothers unless listed otherwise):

Jesse James/Brad/Scott/Bob/Brad/Steve Armstrong (father and brothers)

Mike/Ted DiBaise (father and son)

Terry/Dory Funk (brothers)

Eddy/Chavo Jr./Chavo Sr./Hector/Mando Guerrero
        (related in a cousin/uncle menagerie)

Bret/Owen/Bulldog/Stu Hart/Jim Neihart
        (brothers, father, and in-laws)

Larry/Curt Hennig (father/son)

Jerry Lawler/Brian Christopher (father and son)

Blackjacks (No relation between the two although father BlackJack
        Mulligan and son Barry Windham were in two versions of this
        team)

Rick/Scott Steiner (brothers)

Ivan/Scott Putiski (father and son)

American Dream/Goldust/Marlena (father, son, divorced wife)

Hulk Hogan/Horace Boulder (uncle/nephew)

Marc Mero/Sable (Married)

Kevin/Nancy Sullivan (Divorced)

DDP/Kimberly (Married)

Tammy Lynn Sytch/Chris Candido
        (Married...I think...but they are a couple)

Steve Austin/Debra (Married)

Vince Sr (Vince Jr's father), Vince Jr, Linda, Shane, Stephanie
        McMahon (Parents, Brother, Sister)

Rocky Maivia/Rocky Johnson/High Chief Peter Maivia
        (Rocky's father and grandfather)

Ric Flair/David Flair (father/son)

Luna Vachon/Gangrel/Maurice/Paul Vachon
        (wife/husband/uncle and father, I think)

Terry/Dory Funk Sr./Dory Funk Jr. (father/sons)

Fritz/Kevin/Mike/Kerry/David/Chris Von Erich (father/sons)

"Professor" Boris Malenko/Dean Malenko (father/son)

Ole/Gene Anderson (in storyline only...not related in real life)

Verne/Greg Gagne (father/son)

Stan/Sean Stasiak (father/son)

Bill/Eric Watts (father/son)

BlackJack Mulligan/Barry/Kendall Windham (father/sons)

Booker T/Stevie Ray (brothers)

Tony/Matt Bourne (father/son)

Randy Savage/Lanny Poffo (Brothers) also Angelo Poffo (father to both)

Doug/Eddie/Mike Gilbert (father/sons)

Bruno/David Sammartino (father/son)

Jack/Jerry Brisco (brothers)

Don/Ron Harris (brothers)

Stan/Larry Zbyszko (No relation)

Finishing Moves

Al Snow:	Snow Plow
Alex Porteau:	Victory Roll
Alex Wright:	German Suplex or Reverse Neckbreaker
Armstrongs, The:	Missile Drop Kick
Atlantis:	Atlantis Lock
Axl Rotten:	SST
Bad Ass Billy Gunn:	FameAsser
Balls Mahoney:	The Nutcracker Suite
Bam Bam Bigelow:	Greetings from Asbury Park
Barbarian:	Kick of Fear
Barry Darsow:	Barely Legal
Barry Horowitz:	Ankle Lock or Horowitz Cradle
Bart Gunn:	Spinning Left Hook
Big Al Greene:	Double Underhook Suplex
Big Dick Dudley:	Total Penetration
Big Sal E. Graziano:	Samoan Drop
Big Show:	Showstopper (Chokeslam)
Blue Meanie:	Meanie-Sault
Bob Holly:	HollyCaust
Bobby Blaze:	Northern Lights Suplex
Bobby Eaton:	Alabama Jam
Booker T:	Harlem Hangover
Brad Armstrong:	Side Russian Leg Sweep

Bradshaw:	Clothesline from Hell
Bret Hart:	Sharpshooter
Brian Adams:	Tilt-a-Whirl Backbreaker or Piledriver
Brian Christopher:	Tennessee Jam
Brian Lee:	Choke Slam
British Bulldog:	Running Powerslam
Buff Bagwell:	Buff Blockbuster
Buh Buh Ray:	Buh Buh Bomb
Bull Pain:	Pain Killer
Cactus Jack:	Double-Arm DDT
Chad Fortune:	Fujiwara Armbar
Chase Tatum:	Backbreaker
Chavo Guerrero Jr:	Tornado DDT
Chris Adams:	Superkick
Chris Benoit:	Crippler Cross-face
Chris Candido:	Blonde Bombshell
Chris Chetti:	Double Springboard Moonsault
Chris Jericho:	Walls of Jericho
Christian:	Impaler/Reverse DDT
Chyna:	The Pedigree
Crash Holly:	Crash course
Curt Hennig:	'Hennig-plex' Fisherman Suplex
Cyclope:	Pendulum Swing
Damien:	Suplex-Neckbreaker
Dave Taylor:	Butterfly Suplex
Dean Malenko:	Texas Cloverleaf
Diamond Dallas Page:	Diamond Cutter
Disciple:	Apocalypse
Disco Inferno:	The Last Dance
Disorderly Conduct:	Double Axhandle/Neckbreaker Combo
D'Lo Brown:	"Lo-down" Frogsplash or Sky-high Powerbomb
Doc Dean:	Missile Dropkick
Doug Furnas:	Power Hoist
Droz:	Jumping Bomb
Dude Love:	Sweet Shin Music followed by Double-Arm DDT
Dudley Boyz:	Dudley Death Drop (3D's)
D-Von Dudley:	Reverse DDT
Eddy Guerrero:	Frogsplash
Edge:	Downward Spiral/Spear
El Dandy:	Mahistral Cradle or the Hand of Stone
El Vampiro:	Nail in the Coffin

Eric Bischoff:	Crescent Kick
Ernest 'The Cat' Miller:	The Feliner
Evan Kourageous:	Kourageous corkscrew moonsault
Faarooq:	Dominator
Fidel Sierra:	Castro Sleeper
Fit Finley:	Tombstone Piledriver
Gangrel:	Impaler DDT
Gedo:	Gedo Clutch or WAR Special
Glacier:	Cryonic Kick
Godfather:	Pimp Drop (Death Valley Driver)
Goldberg:	Jackhammer
Goldust:	Curtain Call
Great Muta:	Moonsault or Green Mist into Eyes
Hardbody Harrison:	Double Underhook DDT
Hardwork Bobby Walker:	Quittin' Time
Hardy Boyz:	Leg Drop/Splash Combo
Headbangers:	Stagedive
Hector Garza:	Standing Moonsault
High Voltage:	Power Surge
Hiro Saito:	Top-Rope Senton
Hiroyoshi Tenzan:	Diving Headbutt
Horace Boulder:	Full Nelson Slam
Horshu:	Rope-Walk Elbow Drop
Hugh Morrus:	'No Laughing Matter' Moonsault
Hulk Hogan:	Atomic Leg Drop
Hunter Hearst Helmsley:	The Pedigree
Jeff Hardy:	Swanton Bomb (Senton bomb)
Jerry Flynn:	Cross Arm-Breaker
Jerry Lynn:	Tombstone
Jim Duggan:	"3-Point Stance" Tackle or Old Glory Knee Drop
Jim Neidhart:	Powerslam
Jim Powers:	Powerslam
John Kronus:	450 Splash
John Nord:	Camel Clutch
Johnny Grunge:	Spinebuster
Johnny Swinger:	Somersault Leg Drop
Jumpin Joey Maggs:	Enziguiri
Justin Credible:	That's Credible (Reverse Corkscrew Piledriver)
Juventud Guerrera:	450 Splash or Juvi Driver
Kane:	Tombstone Piledriver/Chokeslam
Kanyon:	The Flatliner

Kaz Hayashi:	Back Body Bomb (Senton Back Splash)
Ken Shamrock:	Ankle Lock Submission
Kendall Windham:	Lariat O'Doom or the Mulligan
Kenny Kaos:	Power Surge
Kevin Nash:	Jack-knife Powerbomb
Kidman:	Shooting Star Press
Konnan:	Tequila Sunrise
Kurt Angle:	Fallaway slam
La Parka:	Top-Rope Body Splash, Chair Shot or Moonsault
Lance Storm:	Leaping Side Kick
Larry Zbyszko:	Larry Land Dreamer
Len Denton:	Superplex
Lenny Lane:	Memory Lane (Full Nelson Slam)
Lex Luger:	Torture Rack
Little Dragon:	Top-Rope Somersault Hurricanrana
Lizmark Jr:	Asai Moonsault (Cartwheel Moonsault)
Lodi:	Spinning DDT
Lorenzo:	Bridge Suplex or Top-Rope Sunset Flip
Luna:	Luna Eclipse
Macho Man Randy Savage:	Flying Elbow Drop
Mankind:	Mandible Claw (Mr. Socko)
Mark Henry:	Big Splash or Powerslam
Mark Star:	Shooting Starr
Marty Jannetty:	Show Stopper
Masa Chono:	STF
Masato Tanaka:	Roaring Elbow or Tornado DDT
Matt Hardy:	Twist of Fate
Mean Mike:	Reverse Neckbreaker
Meng:	Tongan Death Grip
Mideon:	Reverse DDT
Mike Awesome:	Awesome Bombs
Mike Enos:	Whirly Bird
Mikey Whipwreck:	Whippersnapper
Mr. Wallstreet:	Stock Market Crash
Mr. World Class Chip Minton:	Brainbuster or Standing Splash
New Jack:	Gangsta Splash
Nick Dinsmore:	Top-Rope Splash
911:	Choke Slam
Norman Smiley:	Norman Conquest
NWO Sting (aka Cobra):	DDT
Ohara:	Praying Powerbomb

Pat Tanaka:	Rolling Kick
Pete Gas:	Gas mask
Pitbulls, The:	Powerbomb
Psicosis:	Guillotine Leg Drop
Public Enemy:	Drive-By
Rage:	Blackout
Raven:	Even Flow DDT
Reese:	Two-Handed Choke Slam
Renegade:	Backbreaker
Rey Misterio, Jr:	Top Rope Hurricanrana
Ric Flair:	Figure-4 Leg Lock
Rick Fuller:	Fuller Effect (K-Driller)
Rick Steiner:	Top-Rope Bulldog
Riggs:	Five Arm or No Remorse
Rikishi Phatu:	Rikishi drop
Road Dogg:	Pump Handle Slam
Roadblock:	Dead End Splash
Rob Van Dam:	Van Daminator or Split Legged Moonsault
Rock, The:	Rock Bottom or People's Elbow
Rocco Rock:	Drive-By
Roddy Piper:	Sleeperhold
Sabu:	Triple Jump Moonsault
Sandman, The:	DDT
Saturn:	Death Valley Driver
Scott Armstrong:	Superkick
Scott D'Amour:	Gedo Clutch Pin
Scott Hall:	Outsiders Edge
Scott Norton:	Powerbomb or Shoulder-buster
Scott Putski:	Putski Bomb
Scott Steiner:	Steiner Recliner
Scott Taylor:	Victory Roll
Sgt. Buddy Lee Parker:	Flying Knee Drop
Shane Douglas:	Belly-to-Belly Suplex
Shawn Michaels:	Sweet Chin Music
Sickboy:	The Cure
Silver King:	Somersault Leg Drop
Spike Dudley:	Acid Drop
Steve Armstrong:	Missile Dropkick
Steve Blackman:	The Guillotine
Steven Regal:	Regal Stretch
Stevie Ray:	Slapjack

Stevie Richards:	Stevie Kick
Sting:	Scorpion Death Drop or Scorpion Death Lock
Stone Cold Steve Austin:	Stone Cold Stunner
Sumo Fuji:	Dragon Suplex
Super Calo:	Top-Rope Ankle Scissors
Super Nova and Blue Meanie:	Blue Light Special
Supernova:	Novacaine
Taka Michinoku:	Michinoku Driver
Tazz:	Tazzmission
Thrasher:	Moonsault or a Top-Rope Leg Drop
Tokyo Magnum:	Air Tokyo
Tommy Dreamer:	DDT
Tommy Rogers:	Tomikaze
Triple H:	The Pedigree
Tuff Tom:	Flying Axehandle
Ultimo Dragon:	Dragon Sleeper
Undertaker:	Tombstone Piledriver
Val Venis:	Money's Hot
Van Hammer:	Flashback
Villano IV:	Flying Cross-Body Block or Standing Leg Drop
Villano V:	Flying Cross-Body Block or Standing Leg Drop
Vincent:	Cobra Clutch or an Arm Bar
Viscera:	Viscera splash
Warrior, The:	Gorilla Press/Big Splash
Wrath:	Meltdown
X-Pac:	X-Factor (Face Buster)
Yuji Nagata:	Nagata-lock

WCW TITLE HISTORY
Major Titles Only

WCW US Title (Combined with WWF IC Title)

Won By	Won From	Date
Lex Luger	Vacant	12/16/90
Sting	Vacant	08/25/91
Rick Rude	Sting	11/19/91
Dustin Rhodes	Vacant	01/11/93
Dustin Rhodes	Vacant	08/30/93
Steve Austin	Dustin Rhodes	12/27/93
Rick Steamboat	Steve Austin	08/24/94
Steve Austin	Vacant	09/18/94
Jim Duggan	Steve Austin	09/18/94
Big Van Vader	Jim Duggan	12/27/94
Sting	Vacant	06/18/94
Kensuke Sasaki	Sting	11/13/95
One Man Gang	Vacant	12/27/95
Konnan	One Man Gang	01/29/96
Ric Flair	Vacant	07/07/96
Eddy Guerrero	Vacant	12/29/96
Dean Malenko	Eddy Guerrero	03/16/97
Jeff Jarrett	Dean Malenko	06/09/97
Steve McMichael	Jeff Jarrett	08/21/97
Curt Hennig	Steve McMichael	09/15/97
DDP	Curt Hennig	12/28/97
Raven	DDP	04/19/98
Bill Goldberg	Raven	04/20/98
Bret Hart	Vacant	07/21/98
Lex Luger	Bret Hart	08/10/98
Bret Hart	Lex Luger	08/13/98
DDP	Bret Hart	10/26/98
Bret Hart	DDP	11/30/98
Roddy Piper	Bret Hart	02/08/99
Scott Hall	Roddy Piper	02/21/99
Scott Steiner	Vacant	04/11/99
David Flair	Vacant	07/05/99
Chris Benoit	David Flair	08/09/99

Sid	Chris Benoit	09/12/99
Goldberg	Sid	10/24/99
Bret Hart	Goldberg	10/25/99
Scott Hall	Bret Hart/Goldberg/Sid	11/08/99
Chris Benoit	Jeff Jarrett	12/19/99
Jeff Jarrett	Chris Benoit	12/20/99
Jeff Jarrett	Vacant	01/17/00
Scott Steiner	Sting	04/16/00
Lance Storm	Tournament	07/18/00
General Rection	Lance Storm	10/29/00
Lance Storm	General Rection	11/13/00
General Rection	Lance Storm	11/26/00
The Franchise	S. Douglas/General Rection	01/14/01
Rick Steiner	Franchise/Shane Douglas	02/05/01
Booker T	Rick Steiner	03/18/01
Kanyon	Vacant	07/??/01
Tajiri	Kanyon	09/10/01
Rhyno	Tajiri	09/10/01
Kurt Angle (WWF)	Rhyno	11/12/01
Edge (WWF)	Kurt Angle	10/22/01

WCW World Title (Renamed World Title in the WWF)

Title Holder	Won From	Date Won
Ric Flair	Sting (NWA)	01/11/91
Lex Luger	Vacant	07/14/91
Sting	Lex Luger	02/29/92
Big Van Vader	Sting	07/12/92
Ron Simmons	Big Van Vader	08/02/92
Big Van Vader	Ron Simmons	12/30/92
Sting	Big Van Vader	03/11/93
Big Van Vader	Sting	03/17/93
Ric Flair	Big Van Vader	12/27/93
Ric Flair	Vacant	04/24/94
Hulk Hogan	Ric Flair	07/17/94
The Giant	Hulk Hogan	10/29/95
Randy Savage	Vacant	11/26/95
Ric Flair	Randy Savage	12/27/95
Randy Savage	Ric Flair	01/22/96
Ric Flair	Randy Savage	02/11/96

The Giant	Ric Flair	04/22/96
Hollywood Hogan	The Giant	08/10/96
Lex Luger	Hollywood Hogan	08/04/97
Hollywood Hogan	Lex Luger	08/09/97
Sting	Hollywood Hogan	12/28/97
Sting	Vacant	02/22/98
Randy Savage	Randy Savage	04/19/98
Hollywood Hogan	Randy Savage	04/20/98
Bill Goldberg	Hollywood Hogan	07/06/98
Kevin Nash	Bill Goldberg	12/27/98
Hollywood Hogan	Kevin Nash	01/04/99
Ric Flair	Hollywood Hogan	03/14/99
DDP	Ric Flair	04/11/99
Sting	DDP	04/26/99
DDP	Sting	04/26/99
Kevin Nash	DDP	05/09/99
Randy Savage	Kevin Nash	07/11/99
Hollywood Hogan	Randy Savage	07/12/99
Sting	Hollywood Hogan	09/12/99
Goldberg	Sting	10/24/99
Bret Hart	Chris Benoit	11/21/99
Bret Hart	Goldberg	12/20/99
Chris Benoit	Sid	01/22/00
Sid	Kevin Nash	01/24/00
Sid	Kevin Nash	01/26/00
Jeff Jarrett	DDP	04/16/00
David Arquette	Eric Bischoff	04/26/00
Jeff Jarrett	David Arquette & DDP	05/7/00
Ric Flair	Jeff Jarrett	05/15/00
Jeff Jarrett	Kevin Nash	05/22/00
Kevin Nash	Jeff Jarrett/Scott Steiner	05/24/00
Ric Flair	Kevin Nash (Handed it over to Flair)	05/29/00
Jeff Jarrett	Ric Flair	05/29/00
Hulk Hogan (Won fake belt)	Jeff Jarrett	07/9/00
Booker T	Jeff Jarrett	07/9/00
Kevin Nash	Booker T	08/28/00
Booker T	Kevin Nash	09/17/00
Booker T	Won in 49ers match	10/2/00
Scott Stiener	Booker T	11/26/00
Booker T	Scott Stiener	03/26/01
Kurt Angle (WWF)	Booker T	07/26/01

105

Booker T	Kurt Angle (WWF)	07/30/01
The Rock (WWF)	Booker T	08/19/01
Chris Jericho (WWF)	The Rock (WWF)	10/21/01
The Rock (WWF)	Chris Jericho (WWF)	11/05/01

WCW Tag Title (Combined with WWF Tag Title)

Won By	Won From	Date
Doom	Vacant	05/19/90
Fabulous Freebirds	Doom	02/24/91
The Steiners	Fabulous Freebirds	02/18/91
Arn Anderson/Larry Zybysko	The Steiners	09/05/91
Rick Steamboat/Dustin Rhodes	Arn Anderson/Larry Zbyszko	11/19/91
Arn Anderson/Bobby Eaton	Steamboat/Dustin Rhodes	01/16/92
The Steiners	Arn Anderson/Bobby Eaton	05/03/92
Terry Gordy/Steve Williams	The Steiners	07/05/92
Barry Windham/Dustin Rhodes	Terry Gordy/Steve Williams	09/21/92
Rick Steamboat/Shane Douglas	Barry Windham/Dustin Rhodes	11/18/92
The Hollywood Blonds	Rick Steamboat/Shane Douglas	03/02/93
Arn Anderson/Paul Roma	The Hollywood Blonds	08/18/93
Nasty Boys	Arn Anderson/Paul Roma	09/19/93
Marcus Bagwell/2 Cold Scorpio	Nasty Boys	10/04/93
Nasty Boys	Marcus Bagwell/2 Cold Scorpio	10/24/93
Cactus Jack/Kevin Sullivan	Nasty Boys	05/22/94
Pretty Wonderful	Cactus Jack/Kevin Sullivan	07/17/94
Stars/Stripes	Pretty Wonderful	09/25/94
Pretty Wonderful	Stars/Stripes	10/23/94
Stars/Stripes	Pretty Wonderful	11/16/94
Harlem Heat	Stars/Stripes	12/08/94
Nasty Boys	Harlem Heat	05/21/95
Harlem Heat	Nasty Boys	06/24/95
Bunkhouse Buck & Dick Slater	Harlem Heat	07/22/95
Harlem Heat	Bunkhouse Buck/Dick Slater	09/17/95
The American Males	Harlem Heat	09/18/95
Harlem Heat	The American Males	09/27/95
Sting/Lex Luger	Harlem Heat	01/22/96
Harlem Heat	Sting/Lex Luger	06/24/96
The Steiners	Harlem Heat	07/24/96
Harlem Heat	The Steiners	07/27/96

Public Enemy	Harlem Heat	09/23/96
Harlem Heat	Public Enemy	09/28/96
The Outsiders	Harlem Heat	10/27/96
The Stieners	The Outsiders	01/25/97
The Outsiders	The Stieners	01/27/97
Giant/Lex Luger	The Outsiders	02/23/97
The Outsiders	Giant/Lex Luger	02/25/97
The Steiners	The Outsiders	10/06/97
The Outsiders	The Steiners	01/12/98
The Steiners	The Outsiders	02/09/98
The Outsiders	The Steiners	02/22/98
Sting/The Giant	The Outsiders	05/17/98
Scott Hall/The Giant	Sting/The Giant	07/21/98
Rick Steiner/Kaos	Scott Steiner/The Giant	10/25/98
Curt Hennig/Barry Windham	Vacant	02/21/99
Benoit/Dean Malenko	Curt Hennig/Barry Windham	03/14/99
Kidman/Rey Mysterio Jr.	Chris Benoit/Dean Malenko	03/29/99
Raven/Saturn	Rey Misterio Jr/Kidman	05/09/99
DDP/Bam Bam Bigelow	Saturn/Kanyon	05/31/99
Saturn/Benoit	Bam Bam/DDP	06/10/99
DDP/Kanyon	Saturn/Benoit	06/13/99
Harlem Heat	DDP/Kanyon	08/14/99
Windhams	Harlem Heat	08/23/99
Harlem Heat	Windhams	09/12/99
Filthy Animals	Harlem Heat	10/18/99
Harlem Heat	Filthy Animals/1st Family	10/24/99
Filthy Animals	Harlem Heat	10/25/99
Creative Control	Filthy Animals	11/22/99
Bret Hart & Goldberg	Creative Control	12/9/99
Outsiders	Bret Hart & Goldberg	12/13/99
David Flair & Crowbar	Kevin Nash & Scott Steiner	1/19/00
Mamalukes	David Flair & Crowbar	1/19/00
The Harris Boys	Mamalukes	02/12/00
Mamalukes	The Harris Boys	02/13/00
The Harris Boys	Mamalukes	03/19/00
Shane Douglas & Buff Bagwell	Ric Flair & Lex Luger	04/16/00
Kronic	Shane Douglas & Buff Bagwell	05/15/00
Chuck Palumbo & Sean Stasiak	Kronic	05/31/00
The Great Muta & Vampiro	Kronic	08/13/00
Rey & Juvi	The Great Muta & Vampiro	08/14/00
Sean O'Haire and Mark Jindrak	Won In Battle Royal	09/25/00

MIA (Chavo and Col. Cajun)	Sean O'Haire and Mark Jindrak	10/11/00
Sean O'Haire and Mark Jindrak	MIA (Chavo and Col. Cajun)	10/11/00
Boogie Knights	Sean O'Haire and Mark Jindrak	11/16/00
Perfect Event	Boogie Knights	11/20/00
Kevin Nash & DDP	Perfect Event	11/26/00
Perfect Event	Kevin Nash & DDP	11/27/00
InSiders (Kevin Nash & DDP)	Perfect Event	12/17/00
Sean O'Haire & Chuck Palumbo	InSiders (Kevin Nash & DDP)	01/14/01
Undertaker/Kane	Sean O'Haire & Chuck Palumb	08/09/01
Booker T/Test	Undertaker/Kane (WWF)	09/25/01
Hardy Boyz (WWF)	Booker T/Test	10/08/01
Dudley Boyz	Hardy Boyz (WWF)	10/25/01

WCW Cruiserweight Title
(Combined with WWF Light Heavyweight Title)

Won By	Won From	Date
Shinjiro Ohtani	Vacant	03/20/96
Dean Malenko	Shinjiro Ohtani	05/02/96
Rey Misterio Jr.	Dean Malenko	07/08/96
Dean Malenko	Rey Misterio Jr.	10/27/96
Ultimo Dragon	Dean Malenko	12/29/96
Dean Malenko	Ultimo Dragon	01/21/97
Syxx	Dean Malenko	02/23/97
Chris Jericho	Syxx	06/28/97
Alex Wright	Chris Jericho	07/28/97
Chris Jericho	Alex Wright	08/16/97
Eddy Guerrero	Chris Jericho	09/14/97
Rey Misterio Jr.	Eddy Guerrero	10/26/97
Eddy Guerrero	Rey Misterio Jr.	11/10/97
Ultimo Dragon	Eddy Guerrero	12/30/97
Juventud Guerrera	Ultimo Dragon	01/08/98
Rey Misterio Jr.	Juventud Guerrera	01/15/98
Chris Jericho	Rey Misterio Jr.	01/24/98
Dean Malenko	Chris Jericho	05/17/98
Chris Jericho	Title Vacated	06/15/98
Rey Misterio Jr.	Chris Jericho	07/12/98
Chris Jericho	Vacant	07/13/98
Juventud Guerrera	Chris Jericho	08/08/98

Kidman	Juventud Guerrera	09/14/98
Juventud Guerrera	Kidman	11/16/98
Kidman	Juventud Guerrera	11/22/98
Rey Misterio Jr.	Kidman	03/15/98
Psicosis	Rey Misterio Jr	04/19/99
Rey Misterio Jr.	Psicosis	04/26/99
Lenny Lane	Rey Misterio Jr.	08/19/99
Psychosis	Vacant	10/04/99
Disco Inferno	Psicosis	10/04/99
Evan Karagias	Disco Inferno	11/21/99
Madusa	Evan Karagias	12/19/99
Oklahoma	Madusa	12/19/99
The Artist	Lash Leroux	02/20/00
Billy Kidman	The Artist	03/30/00
The Artist	Billy Kidman	03/31/00
Chris Candido	Won 6 Man Title Tournament	04/16/00
Crowbar	Chris Candido	05/15/00
Daffney	Crowbar	05/22/00
Lt. Loco	Daffney & Disco Inferno	06/7/00
Lance Storm	Lt. Loco	07/31/00
Elix Skipper	Lance Storm (Handed belt over	08/14/00
Mike Sanders	Elix Skipper	10/2/00
Chavo Guerrero	Mike Sanders	12/6/00
Shane Helms	Chavo Guerrero	03/18/01
Billy Kidman	Gregory Helms	07/05/01
X-Pac (WWF)	Billy Kidman	07/30/01
Billy Kidman	X-Pac (WWF)	10/11/01
Tajiri (WWF)	Billy Kidman	10/22/01

WWF TITLE HISTORY
(Current Major Titles Only)

WWF World Title

Champion	Won from	Date Won
Buddy Rogers	Nobody	01/24/63
Bruno Sammartino	Buddy Rogers	05/17/63
Ivan Koloff	Bruno Sammartino	01/18/71
Pedro Morales	Ivan Koloff	02/08/71
Stan Staisak	Pedro Morales	12/01/73
Bruno Sammartino	Stan Staisak	12/10/73
Billy Graham	Bruno Sammartino	04/30/77
Bob Backlund	Billy Graham	02/20/78
Antonio Inoki	Bob Backlund	11/30/79
Bob Backlund	Antonio Inoki	12/06/79
The Iron Sheik	Bob Backlund	11/23/81
Hulk Hogan	The Iron Sheik	12/26/83
Andre the Giant	Hulk Hogan	02/05/88
Randy Savage	Ted DiBiase	03/27/88
Hulk Hogan	Randy Savage	04/02/89
Ultimate Warrior	Hulk Hogan	04/01/90
Sgt. Slaughter	Ultimate Warrior	01/19/91
Hulk Hogan	Sgt. Slaughter	03/24/91
Undertaker	Hulk Hogan	11/27/91
Hulk Hogan	Undertaker	12/03/91
Ric Flair	Nobody	01/19/92
Randy Savage	Ric Flair	04/05/92
Ric Flair	Randy Savage	09/01/92
Bret Hart	Ric Flair	10/12/92
Yokozuna	Bret Hart	04/04/93
Hulk Hogan	Yokozuna	04/04/93
Yokozuna	Hulk Hogan	06/13/93
Bret Hart	Yokozuna	03/20/94
Bob Backlund	Bret Hart	11/23/94
Diesel	Bob Backlund	11/26/94
Bret Hart	Diesel	11/19/95
Shawn Michaels	Bret Hart	03/31/96
Sycho Sid	Shawn Michaels	11/17/96

HBK	Sycho Sid	01/19/97
Bret Hart	4 Way Match	02/16/97
Sycho Sid	Bret Hart	02/17/97
The Undertaker	Sycho Sid	03/23/97
Bret Hart	Undertaker	08/06/97
HBK	Bret Hart	11/09/97
Steve Austin	HBK	03/24/98
Kane	Steve Austin	06/28/98
Steve Austin	Kane	06/29/98
Rocky Maivia	Nobody	10/15/98
Mankind	Rocky Maivia	01/04/99
Rocky Maivia	Mankind	01/24/99
Mankind	Rocky Maivia	01/31/99
Rocky Maivia	Mankind	02/15/99
Steve Austin	Rocky Maivia	03/28/99
Undertaker	Steve Austin	05/23/99
Steve Austin	Undertaker	06/28/99
Mankind	Steve Austin	08/22/99
Triple H	Mankind	08/23/99
Vince McMahon	Triple H	09/16/99
Triple H	(Won Six-Pac Match)	09/26/99
The Big Show	Triple H/The Rock	11/14/99
Triple H	The Big Show	01/3/00
The Rock	Triple H	04/30/00
Triple H	The Rock	05/21/00
The Rock	Triple H (Vince McMahon)	06/26/00
Kurt Angle	The Rock	10/22/00
The Rock	Kurt Angle	02/25/01
Steve Austin	The Rock	04/01/01
Kurt Angle	Steve Austin (WCW)	09/23/01
Steve Austin (WCW)	Kurt Angle	10/08/01

WWF Intercontinental Title

Champion	Won From	Date Won
Pat Patterson	Vacant	9/11/79
Ken Patera	Pat Patterson	4/21/80
Pedro Morales	Ken Patera	12/8/80
Don Muraco	Pedro Morales	6/20/81
Pedro Morales	Don Muraco	11/23/81
Tito Santana	Pedro Morales	1/23/83
Greg Valentine	Tito Santana	2/11/84
Tito Santana	Greg Valentine	9/24/84
Randy Savage	Tito Santana	7/5/85
Ricky Steamboat	Randy Savage	2/8/86
Honky Tonk Man	Ricky Steamboat	3/29/87
Ultimate Warrior	Honkey Tonk Man	8/29/88
Rick Rude	Ultimate Warrior	4/2/89
Ultimate Warrior	Rick Rude	8/28/89
Mr. Perfect	Vacant	4/23/90
Texas Tornado	Mr. Perfect	8/27/90
Mr. Perfect	Texas Tornado	11/19/90
Bret Hart	Mr. Perfect	8/26/91
The Mountie	Bret Hart	1/17/92
Roddy Piper	The Mountie	1/19/92
Bret Hart	Roddy Piper	4/5/92
Davey Boy Smith	Bret Hart	8/29/92
Shawn Michaels	Davey Boy Smith	10/27/92
Marty Jannetty	Shawn Michaels	5/17/93
Shawn Michaels	Marty Jannetty	6/6/93
Razor Ramon	Vacant	9/27/93
Diesel	Razor Ramon	4/13/94
Razor Ramon	Diesel	8/29/94
Jeff Jarrett	Razor Ramon	1/22/95
Razor Ramon	Jeff Jarrett	5/19/96
Jeff Jarrett	Razor Ramon	5/21/95
Shawn Michaels	Jeff Jarrett	7/23/95
Dean Douglas	Vacant	10/22/95
Razor Ramon	Dean Douglas	10/22/95
Goldust	Razor Ramon	1/21/96
Ahmed Johnson	Goldust	6/23/96
Triple H	Marc Mero	10/21/96
Rocky Maivia	Triple H	2/13/97

Owen Hart	Rocky Maivia	4/28/97
Steve Austin	Owen Hart	8/6/97
Owen Hart	Vacant	10/5/97
Steve Austin	Steve Austin	8/3/97
Rocky Maivia	Vacant	12/8/97
Triple H	Rocky Maivia	8/30/98
Ken Shamrock	Vacant	10/12/98
Val Venis	Ken Shamrock	2/14/99
Road Dog	Val Venis	3/15/99
Goldust	Road Dog	3/29/99
Godfather	Goldust	4/12/99
Jeff Jarrett	Godfather	5/31/99
Edge	Jeff Jarrett	6/23/99
Jeff Jarrett	Edge	6/25/99
D-Lo Brown	Jeff Jarrett	8/2/99
Jeff Jarrett	D-Lo Brown	8/22/99
Chyna	Jeff Jarrett	10/17/99
Chris Jericho	Chyna	10/17/99
Chris Jericho & Chyna	Decision of WWF officials	1/3/00
Chris Jericho	Chyna & Hardcore Holly	1/23/00
Kurt Angle	Chris Jericho	2/27/00
Chris Benoit	Kurt Angle & Chris Jericho	4/02/00
Chris Jericho	Chris Benoit	5/04/00
Chris Benoit	Chris Jericho	5/08/00
Rikishi	Chris Benoit	6/22/00
Val Venis	Rikishi	7/06/00
Chyna	Val Venis	8/27/00
Eddy G.	Chyna	9/04/00
Billy Gunn	Eddy G.	11/23/00
Chris Benoit	Billy Gunn	12/10/00
Chris Jericho	Chris Benoit	01/21/01
Triple H	Chris Jericho	04/05/01
Jeff Hardy	Triple H	04/12/01
Triple H	Jeff Hardy	04/16/01
Kane	Triple H	05/20/01
Albert	Kane	06/28/01
Lance Storm	Albert	07/23/01
Edge	Lance Storm	08/19/01
Christian	Edge	09/23/01
Edge	Christian (WCW)	10/21/01
Test(WCW)	Edge	11/05/01
Edge	Test (WCW)	11/18/01

WWF Tag Team Title

Champion	Won From	Date Won
Luke Graham/Tarzan Tyler	Vacant	1971
Karl Gotch/Rene Goulet	Luke Graham/Tarzan Tyler	12/6/71
Baron Mikel Scicluna/ King Curtis Iaukea	Karl Gotch/Rene Goulet	2/1/72
Sonny King/Chief Jay Strongbow	Baron Mikel Scicluna/ King Curtis Iaukea	5/22/72
Toru Tanaka/Mr. Fuji	Sonny King/Chief Jay Strongbow	6/27/72
Tony Garea/Haystacks Calhoun	Toru Tanaka/Mr. Fuji	5/30/73
Toru Tanaka/Mr. Fuji	Tony Garea/Haystacks Calhoun	9/11/73
Tony Garea/Dean Ho	Toru Tanaka/Mr. Fuji	11/14/73
Jimmy Valiant/Johnny Valiant	Tony Garea/Dean Ho	5/8/74
Dominic Denucc/Victor Rivera	Jimmy Valiant/Johnny Valiant	5/13/75
Dominic Denucci/Pat Barrett	Vacant	1975
Blackjack Lanza/Blackjack Mulligan	Dominic Denucci/Pat Barrett	8/26/75
Tony Parisi/Louis Cerda	Blackjack Lanza/Blackjack Mulligan	11/18/75
Executioners	Tony Parisi/Louis Cerdan	5/76/11
Chief Jay Strongbow/ Billy White Wolf	Vacant	12/7/76
Toru Tanaka/Mr. Fuji	Vacant	9/27/77
Dominic Denucci/Dino Bravo	Toru Tanaka/Mr. Fuji	3/14/78
Yukon Lumberjacks	Dominic Denucci/Dino Bravo	6/26/78
Tony Garea/Larry Zbyszko	Yukon Lumberjacks	11/21/78
Johnny Valiant/Jerry Valiant	Tony Garea/Larry Zbyszko	3/6/79
Ivan Putski/Tito Santana	Johnny Valiant/Jerry Valiant	10/22/79
Samoans	Ivan Putski/Tito Santana	4/12/80
Bob Backlund/Pedro Morales	Samoans	8/9/80
Samoans	Vacant	9/9/80
Tony Garea/Rick Martel	Samoans	11/8/80
Moondogs	Tony Garea/Rick Martel	3/17/81
Moondogs	Vacant	1981
Tony Garea/Rick Martel	Moondogs	7/21/81
Mr. Fuji/Mr. Saito	Tony Garea/Rick Martel	10/13/81
Chief Jay Strongbow/ Jules Strongbow	Mr. Fuji & Mr. Saito	6/28/82
Mr. Fuji & Mr. Saito	Chief Jay Strongbow/ Jules Strongbow	7/13/82
Chief Jay Strongbow/ Jules Strongbow	Mr. Fuji & Mr. Saito	10/26/82
Samoans	Chief Jay Strongbow/ Jules Strongbow	3/8/83
Rocky Johnson/Tony Atlas	Samoans	11/15/83
North-South Connection	Rocky Johnson/Tony Atlas	4/17/84
Mike Rotundo/Barry Windham	North-South Connection	1/21/85
Iron Sheik/Nikolai Volkoff	Mike Rotundo/Barry Windham	3/31/85
US Express	Iron Sheik/Nikolai Volkoff	6/17/85

Dream Team	US Express	8/24/85
British Bulldogs	Dream Team	4/7/86
Hart Foundation	British Bulldogs	1/26/87
Strike Force	Hart Foundation	10/17/87
Demolition	Strike Force	3/27/88
Brainbusters	Demolition	7/18/89
Demolition	Brainbusters	10/2/89
Colossal Connection	Demolition	12/13/89
Demolition	Collossal Connection	4/1/90
Hart Foundation	Demolition	8/27/90
Nasty Boys	Hart Foundation	3/24/91
Legion of Doom	Nasty Boys	8/26/91
Money Inc.	Legion of Doom	2/7/92
Natural Disasters	Money Inc.	7/20/92
Money Inc.	Natural Disasters	10/13/92
Rick Steiner/Scott Steiner	Money Inc.	6/14/93
Money Inc.	Rick Steiner/Scott Steiner	6/16/93
Rick Steiner/Scott Steiner	Money Inc.	6/19/93
Quebecers	Rick Steiner/Scott Steiner	9/13/93
Marty Janetty/1-2-3 Kid	Quebecers	1/10/94
Quebecers	Marty Janetty/1-2-3 Kid	1/17/94
Men On a Mission	Quebecers	3/29/94
Quebecers	Men on a Mission	3/31/94
Headshrinkers	Quebecers	4/26/94
Shawn Michaels/Diesel	Headshrinkers	8/28/94
1-2-3 Kid/Bob Holly	Vacant	1/22/95
Smoking Gunns	1-2-3 Kid/Bob Holly	1/23/95
Owen Hart/Yokozuna	Smoking Gunns	4/2/95
Smoking Gunns	Owen Hart/Yokozuna	9/25/95
Bodydonnas	Vacant	3/31/96
The Godwinns	Bodydonnas	5/19/96
Smoking Gunns	The Godwinns	5/26/96
Owen Hart/Davey Boy Smith	Smoking Gunns	9/22/96
Steve Austin/Shawn Michaels	Owen Hart/Davey Boy Smith	5/26/97
Steve Austin/Dude Love	Vacant	7/14/97
The Headbangers	Vacant	9/7/97
The Godwinns	Headbangers	10/5/97
The Legion of Doom	Godwinns	10/7/97
New Age Outlaws	Legion of Doom	11/24/97
Hardcore Legends	New Age Outlaws	3/29/98
New Age Outlaws	Hardcore Legends	3/30/98
Kane/Mankind	New Age Outlaws	7/13/98
Austin/Undertaker	Kane/Mankind	7/26/98
Kane/Mankind	Austin/Undertaker	8/10/98
New Age Outlaws	Kane/Mankind	8/30/98
Shamrock/Boss Man	New Age Outlaws	12/14/98
Jarrett/Owen Hart	Shamrock/Big Boss Man	1/25/99
Kane/X-Pac	Jarrett/Owen Hart	3/30/99

Acolytes	Kane/X-Pac	5/31/99
Hardy Boys	Acolytes	6/5/99
Acolytes	Hardy Boys	7/25/99
Kane/X-Pac	Acolytes	8/16/99
Undertaker/Big Show	Kane/X-Pac	8/22/99
The Rock/Mankind	Undertaker/Big Show	8/22/99
Undertaker/Big Show	The Rock/Mankind	9/9/99
The Rock/Mankind	Undertaker/Big Show	9/20/99
The New Age Outlaws	The Rock/Mankind	9/23/99
The Rock/Mankind	New Age Outlaws	10/15/99
Crash & Hardcore Holly	Rock/Mankind	10/18/99
Al Snow & Mankind	Crash & Hardcore Holly	11/4/99
The New Age Outlaws	Al Snow & Mankind	11/8/99
The Dudley Boyz	The New Age Outlaws	2/27/00
Edge & Christian	The Dudley Boyz/The Hardy Boyz	4/02/00
Too Cool	Edge/Christian	5/29/00
Edge/Christian	Too Cool	6/26/00
Hardy Boyz	Edge/Christian	9/24/00
Los Conquistadors	Hardy Boyz	10/22/00
Hardy Boyz	Edge & Christian	10/23/00
Right To Censor	Hardy Boyz	11/06/00
(Bull & Goodfather)		
Edge & Christian	Right To Censor	12/10/00
Rock & Undertaker	Edge & Christian	12/18/00
Edge & Christian	Rock & Undertaker	12/21/00
Dudley Boyz	Edge & Christian	01/21/01
Hardy Boyz	Dudley Boyz	03/05/01
Edge & Christian	Hardy Boyz	03/19/01
Dudley Boyz	Edge & Christian	03/19/01
Edge & Christian	Dudley Boyz	04/01/01
Undertaker & Kane	Edge & Christian	04/19/01
Steve Austin & Triple H	Undertaker & Kane	04/29/01
Chris Jericho & Chris Benoit	Steve Austin & Triple H	05/21/01
Dudley Boyz	Chris Jericho & Chris Benoit	06/21/01
APA	Dudley Boyz	07/09/01
Kanyon/DDP (WCW)	APA	08/09/01
Undertaker/Kane	Kanyon/DDP (WCW)	08/19/01
Dudley Boyz (WCW)	Undertaker/Kane	09/17/01
Jericho/Rock	Dudley Boyz (WCW)	10/22/01
Test/Booker T (WCW)	Jericho/Rock	11/01/01
Hardy Boyz	Test/Booker T (WCW)	11/01/01
Dudley Boyz (WCW)	Hardy Boys	11/18/01

WWF Lightweight Title

Champion	Defeated	Date Won
Perro Aguayo	Vacant	3/26/81
Fishman	Perro Aguayo	9/25/81
Perro Aguayo	Fishman	10/1/81
Chris Adams	Perro Aguayo	12/13/81
Perro Aguayo	Chris Adams	4/21/82
Gran Hamada	Perro Aguayo	8/29/82
Perro Aguayo	Gran Hamada	3/20/82
Villano III	Perro Aguayo	8/7/83
Perro Aguayo	Villano III	4/17/84
Gran Hamada	Perro Aguayo	5/20/84
Villano III	Gan Hamada	8/24/86
Fishman	Villano III	12/24/86
Perro Aguayo	Vacant	5/03/87
Villano III	Vacant	6/17/87
Rambo	Villano III	10/04/87
Villano III	Rambo	7/11/88
Sangre Chicana	Villano III	8/14/89
Perro Aguayo	Sangre Chicana	10/15/89
Sangre Chicana	Perro Aguayo	12/3/89
Villano III	Sangre Chicana	5/27/90
Pegasus Kid	Villano III	3/3/91
Villano III	Pegasus Kid	9/13/92
El Signo	Villano III	1/1/93
Villano III	El Signo	7/18/94
Aero Flash	Vacant	6/16/95
Great Sasuke	Aero Flash	3/24/96
El Samurai	Great Sasuke	6/22/96
Great Sasuke	Vacant	8/4/96
Ultimo Dragon	Great Sasuke	10/11/96
Jushin Liger	Ultimo Dragon	1/4/97
El Samurai	Jushin Liger	7/6/97
Shinjiro Ohtani	El Samurai	8/10/97
Taka Michinoku	Vacant	12/7/97
Christian	Taka Michinoku	10/18/98
Duane Gill/Gillberg	Christian	11/23/98
Essa Rios	Gillberg	2/13/00
Dean Malenko	Essa Rios	3/13/00
Scotty Too Hotty	Dean Malenko	4/17/00

Dean Malenko	Scotty Too Hotty	4/27/00
Crash Holly	Dean Malenko	03/18/01
Jerry Lynn	Crash Holly	04/29/01
Jeff Hardy	Jerry Lynn	06/07/01
X-Pac	Jeff Hardy	06/25/01
Tajiri	X-Pac	08/06/01
X-Pac	Tajiri	08/19/01

WWF European Title

Champion	Defeated	Date Won
British Bulldog	Vacant	6/2/97
Shawn Michaels	British Bulldog	9/20/97
Triple H	Shawn Michaels	12/11/97
Owen Hart	Vacant	1/20/98
Triple H	Owen Hart	3/15/98
D-Lo Brown	Triple H	7/14/98
X-Pac	D-Lo Brown	9/21/98
D-Lo Brown	X-Pac	10/5/98
X-Pac	D-Lo Brown	10/18/98
Shane McMahon	X-Pac	2/15/99
Mideon	Title Reinstated	7/4/99
D-Lo Brown	Mideon	7/25/99
Jeff Jarrett	D-Lo Brown	8/22/99
Mark Henry	Jeff Jarrett	8/23/99
D-Lo Brown	Mark Henry	9/26/99
British Bulldog	D-Lo Brown	10/26/99
Val Venis	British Bulldog/D-Lo Brown	12/12/99
Kurt Angle	Val Venis	2/10/00
Chris Jericho	Kurt Angle & Chris Benoit	4/02/00
Eddy Guerrero	Chris Jericho	4/03/00
Perry Saturn	Eddy Guerrero	7/23/00
Al Snow	Perry Saturn	8/31/00
William Regal	Al Snow	10/16/00
Crash Holly	William Regal	12/2/00
William Regal	Crash Holly	12/4/00
Test	William Regal	01/22/01
Eddy Guerrero	Test	04/01/01
Matt Hardy	Eddy Guerrero	04/26/01

| Hurricane Helms | Matt Hardy | 08/27/01 |
| Bradshaw | Hurricane Helms | 10/22/01 |

WWF Hardcore Title

Winner	Won from	Date
Mankind	Vacant	11/2/98
Big Boss Man	Mankind	11/30/98
Road Dog	Big Boss Man	12/21/98
Bob Holly	Nobody	2/14/99
Billy Gunn	Bob Holly	3/15/99
Hardcore Holly	Billy Gunn	3/28/99
Al Snow	Hardcore Holly	4/15/99
Bossman	Al Snow	7/25/99
Al Snow	Bossman	8/22/99
Bossman	Al Snow	8/26/99
British Bulldog	Bossman	9/9/99
Al Snow	British Bulldog	9/9/99
Big Bossman	Al Snow	10/12/99
Test	Big Bossman	1/17/00
Crash Holly	Test	2/24/00
Pete Gas	Crash Holly	3/13/00
Crash Holly	Pete Gas	3/13/00
Tazz	Crash Holly	4/02/00
Viscera	Tazz	4/02/00
Sho Funaki	Viscera	4/02/00
Rodney	Sho Funaki	4/02/00
Joey Abs	Rodney	4/02/00
Thrasher	Joey Abs	4/02/00
Pete Gas	Thrasher	4/02/00
Tazz	Pete Gas	4/02/00
Crash Holly	Tazz	4/02/00
Hardcore Holly	Crash Holly	4/02/00
Crash Holly	Hardcore Holly	4/3/00
Perry Saturn	Crash Holly	4/13/00
Tazz	Perry Saturn	4/13/00
Crash Holly	Tazz	4/13/00
Matt Hardy	Crash Holly	4/24/00
Crash Holly	Matt Hardy	4/27/00

British Bulldog	Crash Holly	5/6/00
Crash Holly	British Bulldog	5/11/00
Godfather's Ho	Crash Holly	5/15/00
Crash Holly	Godfather's Ho	5/15/00
Gerald Brisco	Crash Holly	5/18/00
Crash Holly	Gerald Brisco	6/12/00
Gerald Brisco	Crash Holly	6/19/00
Pat Patterson	Gerald Brisco	6/19/00
Crash Holly	Pat Patterson	6/26/00
Steve Blackman	Crash Holly	6/29/00
Shane McMahon	Steve Blackman	8/21/00
Steve Blackman	Shane McMahon	8/27/00
Crash Holly	Steve Blackman	9/24/00
Perry Saturn	Crash Holly	9/24/00
Steve Blackman	Perry Saturn	9/24/00
Raven	Steve Blackman	12/25/00
Al Snow	Raven	01/22/01
Raven	Al Snow	01/22/01
Hardcore Holly	Raven	02/08/01
Raven	Hardcore Holly	02/08/01
Billy Gunn	Raven	02/25/01
Raven	Billy Gunn	02/25/01
Big Show	Raven	02/25/01
Raven	Big Show	03/19/01
Kane	Raven	04/01/01
Rhyno	Kane	04/19/01
Big Show	Rhyno	05/21/01
Chris Jericho	Big Show	05/28/01
Rhyno	Chris Jericho	05/28/01
Test	Rhyno	06/14/01
Rhyno	Test	06/25/01
Mike Awesome	Rhyno	06/25/01
Jeff Hardy	Mike Awesome	07/11/01
Rob Van Dam	Jeff Hardy	07/22/01
Jeff Hardy	Rob Van Dam	08/13/01
Rob Van Dam	Jeff Hardy	08/19/01
Kurt Angle	Rob Van Dam	09/10/01
Rob Van Dam	Kurt Angle	09/10/01

WWF Women's Title

Winners	Won From	Date Won
Slave Girl Moolah	Vacant	9/18/56
Betty Boucher	Slave Girl Moolah	9/17/66
Fabulous Moolah	Betty Boucher	1966
Yukiko Tomoe	Fabulous Moolah	03/10/68
Fabulous Moolah	Yukiko Tomoe	04/02/68
Sue Green	Fabulous Moolah	1976
Fabulous Moolah	Sue Green	1976
Evelyn Stevens	Fabulous Moolah	10/08/78
Fabulous Moolah	Vacant	10/10/78
Wendi Richter	Fabulous Moolah	07/23/84
Leilani Kai	Wendi Richter	02/18/85
Wendi Richter	Leilani Kai	03/31/85
Fabulous Moolah	Wendi Richter	11/25/85
Velvet McIntyre	Fabulous Moolah	07/03/86
Fabulous Moolah	Velvet McIntyre	07/09/86
Velvet McIntyre	Fabulous Moolah	1986
Fabulous Moolah	Velvet McIntyre	1986
Sherri Martel	Fabulous Moolah	07/24/87
Rockin' Robin	Sherri Martel	10/07/88
Alundra Blaze	Vacant	12/13/93
Bull Nakano	Alundra Blaze	11/20/94
Alundra Blaze	Bull Nakano	04/03/95
Bertha Faye	Alundra Blaza	08/27/95
Alundra Blaze	Bertha Faye	10/23/95
Jacqueline	Vacant	9/15/98
Sable	Jacqueline	11/15/98
Debra	Sable	5/10/99
Ivory	Debra	6/14/99
Fabulous Moolah	Ivory	10/17/99
Ivory	Fabulous Moolah	10/25/99
Miss Kitty	Ivory/B.B./Jacqueline	10/25/99
Harvey Wippleman	The Cat	1/31/00
Jacqueline	Harvey Wippleman	2/3/00
Stephanie McMahon-Helmsley	Jacqueline	2/3/00
Lita	Stephanie McMahon-Helmsley	8/21/00
Ivory	Lita	11/02/00
Chyna	Ivory	04/01/01
Trish Stratus	Battle Royal	11/18/01

OLD SCHOOL ANSWERS
1. D
2. C
3. B. Tor Johnson, who most notably appeared as a zombie in Wood's *Plan Nine From Outer Space* (1959).
4. A
5. C
6. B. It was basically a half-nelson.
7. D
8. C
9. B
10. False. They wrestled for the WWF title but came to a draw after a marathon 54-minute battle.
11. D
12. C
13. A
14. C
15. A
16. B
17. C
18. D
19. A
20. C
21. B
22. D
23. A
24. A
25. C
26. B. The World Wide Wrestling Federation
27. B
28. C
29. D
30. A
31. D
32. B
33. C
34. A
35. D
36. C
37. A
38. C
39. B
40. D
41. D
42. B
43. B
44. D
45. A
46. B
47. B
48. A
49. C
50. D
51. B
52. Dan Spivey
53. A
54. D
55. A
56. C
57. C
58. False. Morales defeated Ivan Koloff and was defeated by Stasiak.
59. False. Adonis and Ventura held the AWA tag team title and Adonis held the WWF tag straps with Dick Murdoch.
60. True
61. True
62. False. They lost the straps to Blackwell and Ken Patera.
63. False. Leilani Kai was the champion. Richter was the challenger.
64. True
65. False. He attacked John Stossel.
66. C
67. B
68. C
69. A
70. A
71. C
72. D
73. True. He held the belt in 1961 with Bob Geigel.
74. True
75. False
76. A
77. A
78. C
79. True
80. D
81. B
82. A
83. C
84. D
85. A
86. B
87. C

INTERNATIONAL ANSWERS
1. B
2. C
3. A
4. B
5. D
6. D
7. C
8. A
9. B
10. D
11. B
12. D
13. B
14. B
15. False. He wrestled as Wild Pegasus.
16. B
17. D
18. C
19. D
20. B
21. True. He defeated Andre on June 17, 1986 in Nagoya, Japan.
22. True
23. False. He was elected in 1995.
24. D

NAME GAME ANSWERS
1. B
2. D
3. C
4. B
5. D
6. A
7. A
8. C
9. D
10. B
11. A
12. C
13. C
14. D
15. B
16. C
17. D
18. F
19. D
20. G
21. True. As The RingMaster he was Ted DiBiase's "Million Dollar Champion."
22. True. He was known as Stunning Steve Austin and teamed with Brian

Pillman in 1993 as The Hollywood Blonds.
23. D
24. C
25. B
26. C
27. A
28. D
29. B
30. D
31. A
32. B
33. C

WCW ANSWERS
1. A. David Arquette. Partnered with Diamond Dallas Page, the two competed against Eric Bischoff and Jeff Jarrett in 2000 and Arquette pinned Bischoff for the title.
2. C
3. C
4. B
5. D
6. C
7. B
8. A
9. D
10. B
11. B
12. C
13. A
14. B
15. A, B, C & D
16. A
17. C
18. True
19. False. Irwin portrayed The Goon, an ex-hockey player.
20. C & A
21. D & E
22. D
23. D
24. B
25. E
26. B & F
27. A, B & D
28. C
29. C
30. A & G
31. B & D
32. C
33. D
34. A
35. F
36. B
37. G
38. E
39. B
40. B
41. C & A. The Mamalukes defeated David Flair & Crowbar.
42. B
43. D
44. D
45. C
46. A
47. A
48. D
49. A
50. D
51. C
52. B
53. A
54. B
55. D
56. C
57. C
58. A
59. A
60. C
61. B
62. A
63. B
64. D
65. C
66. A
67. D
68. A
69. B
70. A
71. A
72. B
73. C
74. B
75. C
76. A
77. D
78. B
79. A
80. C
81. D
82. B
83. A
84. B
85. D
86. True
87. False. 1994
88. True
89. True. They wrestled at Music City Showdown on May 7, 1989.
90. False. He turned on Hogan.
91. False. Piper won.
92. True. He officiated the match between Larry Zbyszko and Eric Bischoff at Starrcade 1997.
93. False
94. False. He wrestled both Ron Simmons and Big Van Vader for the championship.
95. B
96. C
97. D
98. C
99. B
100. A
101. D
102. A
103. C
104. B
105. B
106. C
107. D
108. A
109. D
110. A
111. D
112. C
113. C
114. B
115. B
116. A
117. A
118. D

MISCELLANEOUS ANSWERS

1. C
2. D
3. A
4. B
5. C
6. D
7. B
8. C
9. D
10. A
11. False. It was Brad Armstrong, the NWA Rookie of the Year in 1982.
12. B. Drozdov was able to vomit on command...and did so regularly.
13. C
14. A
15. C
16. B
17. D
18. B
19. C
20. A
21. C
22. B. El Gigante Gonzalez was reported to be 7' 7".
23. D
24. A
25. B
26. D
27. K. Yokozuna beat Bret Hart in April 1993 for the WWF title, then lost the title to Hulk Hogan that same night. Yokozuna regained the title in June 1993 from Hulk Hogan, and kept it until April of the following year.
28. A
29. C
30. B
31. A. Nagurski defeated Lou Thesz in 1939 to win the NWA world belt.
32. D
33. C
34. C
35. F
36. D
37. B
38. True
39. A
40. C
41. A
42. D
43. B
44. C
45. D
46. B
47. C
48. D
49. C
50. A. Ted Irvine played hockey in the NHL.
51. B
52. C
53. A
54. D
55. B
56. True
57. False. He joined up with Colonel Robert Parker.
58. True
59. C
60. B
61. D
62. A
63. D
64. C
65. A
66. B
67. C
68. A
69. B
70. D
71. D
72. False. He wrestled as The Midnight Rider.
73. True
74. False. Bockwinkel won the belt over Hansen by default.
75. True
76. False. He wrestled George Steele at Wrestlemania 2 and Steamboat at Wrestlemania 3.
77. False. He defeated Jim Powers.
78. True, by countout.
79. False. Nitro debuted at the Mall of America in Bloomington, MN.
80. True
81. True
82. False. Mankind won the match.
83. True
84. False. He made his debut at the 1999 Survivor Series.
85. True
86. D
87. B
88. D
89. C
90. B
91. True, in 1996.
92. C
93. D
94. D
95. C, E & F
96. D
97. B & C
98. E
99. C & D
100. B
101. C. Tazz defeated Yoshihiro Tajiri.
102. A
103. A
104. D
105. A
106. B
107. E. Tazz defeated Kronus.
108. B
109. B
110. C
111. A
112. A
113. A
114. C
115. C. Raven defeated The Sandman.
116. C
117. B
118. A
119. A
120. B
121. A
122. D
123. D
124. B
125. D
126. D
127. B
128. A
129. B
130. B
131. C
132. C
133. False
134. False. He was known as "Sodbuster."
135. False. He was known as King Kong Brody.
136. False. Van Dam was stripped of the title due to injury.
137. True
138. False. He turned on Tazz.

124

WWF ANSWERS

1. D
2. C
3. False. The Undertaker beat Kane.
4. True
5. B
6. False. He won the WWF Intercontinental title in 1998 and the European Championship belt in 1999, but never won the Hardcore Championship.
7. A. Mark Henry, who was also known as "Sexual Chocolate."
8. D
9. A, C & D. She was crowned Miss Illinois, Miss Texas USA and was the wife of Steve "Mongo" McMichael of the Chicago Bears.
10. B
11. D
12. C
13. B
14. A
15. C
16. A
17. B
18. D. Chris Jericho defeated Triple H in 2000, then Triple H bullied the referee into reversing the decision.
19. C
20. B
21. F
22. D
23. D
24. A
25. C
26. B
27. A. February 1997
28. B
29. C
30. E
31. D
32. A
33. B, C & D. Steve Austin won.
34. A
35. C. Triple H defeated Owen Hart.
36. F
37. D
38. A
39. B & D
40. C
41. C
42. E & G
43. B
44. A, D, G & H
45. E. Rick Rude defeated Ultimate Warrior.
46. D. Randy Savage defeated George "The Animal" Steele.
47. D. Triple H defeated The Rock.
48. B, E & G. Shawn Michaels won.
49. B
50. A & F
51. B & C. The Ultimate Warrior defeated Randy "Macho King" Savage.
52. B
53. A. Ken Shamrock defeated "Bad Ass" Billy Gunn.
54. E
55. B & D
56. E. Undertaker defeated Vader.
57. A
58. C
59. A
60. D
61. A
62. D
63. B
64. A
65. D
66. A
67. D
68. C
69. A
70. D
71. D
72. B
73. C
74. D
75. A
76. C
77. B
78. A
79. B
80. C
81. A
82. B
83. D
84. A
85. B
86. D
87. A
88. C
89. D
90. True
91. False
92. False. It aired on the USA Network.
93. True
94. False. He wrestled in Summerslam 1989.
95. B
96. C
97. A
98. D
99. B
100. D
101. B

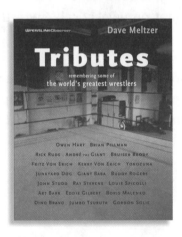
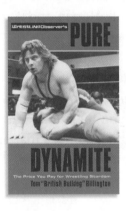

About the Author

Brendan O'Neill, a life-long fan of all sports, became intrigued by professional wrestling in the early 1980s after seeing legends like Hulk Hogan and Andre the Giant on weekly cable wrestling programs.

Brendan, who holds a degree in journalism from Marquette University, has been a sportswriter at various newspapers throughout Illinois and Wisconsin, and was the editor of *Edge Magazine*, a men's magazine from the publishers of *WOW (World of Wrestling) Magazine*.